The
Panel Study
of
Income
Dynamics

GUIDES TO MAJOR SOCIAL SCIENCE DATA BASES

EDITOR
Peter V. Marsden
Harvard University

The purpose of this series is to guide and inform about secondary use of major social science data bases. Each volume serves as a user's guide to one significant, frequently analyzed source of information, reviewing its content, study design, procedures for gaining access to the data sets, and the kinds of analyses that the data can support. The guides will also direct the prospective user to additional documentation of interest, including detailed codebooks and technical reports.

1. **The NORC General Social Survey: A User's Guide**
   James A. Davis
   Tom W. Smith

2. **The Panel Study of Income Dynamics: A User's Guide**
   Martha S. Hill

The
Panel Study
of
Income
Dynamics

A User's Guide

Guides to Major Social Science Data Bases **2**

Martha S. Hill

with assistance of the staff of the PSID

SAGE PUBLICATIONS
The International Professional Publishers
Newbury Park   London   New Delhi

For information address:

 SAGE Publications, Inc.
2455 Teller Road
Newbury Park, California 91320

SAGE Publications Ltd.
6 Bonhill Street
London EC2A 4PU
United Kingdom

SAGE Publications India Pvt. Ltd.
M-32 Market
Greater Kailash I
New Delhi 110 048 India

Printed in the United States of America

Library of Congress Cataloging-in-Publication Data

ISSN 1058-4862

ISBN 0-8039-4609-0 cloth / ISBN 0-8039-4230-3 paper

FIRST PRINTING, 1992

Sage Production Editor: Astrid Virding

Contents

Series Editor's Introduction

In one way of conducting social science research, independent investigators take responsibility for all phases of a research project: After formulating ideas, they collect, analyze, and present evidence. This "holistic" approach was once the dominant style, and, of course, many researchers continue to follow it. In much contemporary research, however, the tasks of data collection and data analysis have come to be separated. Analysts often study information contained in large, multiuser data bases assembled by major survey organizations and government agencies. These data bases are designed to meet multiple purposes and to be of long-term value to the research community. Such large data gathering efforts are generally conducted on a scale that is beyond the capacity of the independent researcher or the small research team; they are expensive and time-consuming.

Much, or even most, analysis of these bodies of information is done by "secondary" researchers other than those responsible for directing "primary" data collection. The separation of data collection from data analysis means, however, that users of a data base must learn about its design and content as well as the research methods used in producing it. Such knowledge is essential to informed secondary analysis. Even the reader of a study based on a large-scale data base may wish to know more about these matters than is provided by the brief summary description of the data typically made available in a research report.

The purpose of this series is to help to diffuse the knowledge required for informed secondary use of major social science data bases. Each volume serves as a user's guide to one significant, frequently analyzed source of information, reviewing its content, study design, sampling plan, and field procedures. Each guide gives details about the various publicly available data sets, produced using information available in the data base, as well as about how to gain access to them; each also illustrates the kinds of analyses that the data base can support. Finally, the guide directs the prospective user to additional documentation of interest, including detailed codebooks and technical reports.

In this guide, Martha S. Hill describes one of the most sustained longitudinal data collection efforts in social science, the Panel Study of Income Dynamics (PSID). Conducted annually since 1968, the PSID has followed 4,800 U.S. households, assembling information on many aspects of the economic and social lives of household members. Because new respondents are added to the PSID as the result of life course events that alter household composition—such as marriages, divorces, births, or changes in residence that lead to the formation of new households—the PSID has, over time, assembled data on more than 37,000 different people. This material is an invaluable source of information for the dynamic study of such topics as wage variations, unemployment, poverty, and participation in transfer programs, among many others. The data are also of great interest to researchers concerned with changes in household structures or life course transitions such as divorce and retirement. Because it represents both individuals and households over a broad time span, the PSID can support diverse research endeavors, both cross-sectional and longitudinal. Hill's clear introduction to the PSID concludes with five examples that illustrate the versatility of this fertile and complex data set together with some of the subtleties involved in making use of it.

—PETER V. MARSDEN, SERIES EDITOR

Foreword

The Panel Study of Income Dynamics began, in 1968, as a poverty study, with a planned lifetime of five years. It was Jim Smith at the Office of Economic Opportunity (OEO) who first suggested to Jim Morgan of the Survey Research Center that he take over a Census Bureau sample already interviewed in the mid-1960s as part of the OEO's Survey of Economic Opportunity and follow them to study "income trajectories." Under Morgan's brilliant leadership, the study benefited from key design decisions (use of a national probability sample of families—nonpoor as well as poor—and following rules designed to keep the sample representative), prudent financial management (Morgan persistently underspent the budget and baffled project sponsors by actually returning unspent funds), a talented and very loyal staff (several of whom are still with us), and good fortune (small and apparently random nonresponse), which made the case for continuing the PSID beyond 1972 irresistible.

Its continuation beyond 1972 was all the more remarkable after its original sponsor, the Office of Economic Opportunity, was unceremoniously put out of business. A delightful, although unsubstantiated, story has it that, when the project was transferred to the Office of the Assistant Secretary for Planning and Evaluation of the Department of Health, Education, and Welfare in 1972, the PSID's dossier contained the note "This is a 10-year study," even though that had never been a stated intention. At any rate, its managers at ASPE, in particular Larry Orr, provided enthusiastic support for the study until the late 1970s, when review panels at the National Science Foundation became convinced that the PSID had outgrown its status as a "poverty study" and had instead become an invaluable general data resource for economists, demographers, and sociologists.

It is surprising that funding commitments for the PSID never extended beyond a single year until its 16th birthday, when a combination of merit (we hope) and bureaucratic exhaustion (we suspect) led to NSF's first multiyear funding. There were a few close calls, especially in the late 1960s, when Guy Orcutt persuaded the OEO and the Urban Institute to help fund the continuation of the nonpoverty portion of the sample, and in the early 1980s, when Reagan's budget ax cut social science funding for the NSF by about one half. Fortunately, a team of private foundations (Ford, Rockefeller, and Sloan) came to our rescue at that point.

Complain as we may, one still has to admire the overall commitment of our nation to support social science data collection projects such as the PSID. Indeed, it was only in the 1980s that European countries—Germany (West and, beginning in 1990, East), the Netherlands, Luxembourg, Ireland, France, and, beginning in 1991, Great Britain—began collecting similar data.

What has all of the money actually bought? The accumulated fruits of the labors of hundreds of people collecting and processing PSID data have produced enough paper to fill the equivalent of several hundred filing cabinets and enough data to fill several reels of computer tape and, beginning with the 1987 files, two CD-ROMs. Taken together, the data provide a fascinating historical record, now extending from the 1960s into the 1990s, of the economic and demographic turmoil in which ordinary American families find themselves—but that they seem to consider quite unremarkable.

This turmoil complicates our lives as producers of the data and yours as analysts of it. But it also helps to dismantle our stereotypes and enrich our theories by forcing us to dig deeper in examining the nature and causes of behavior.

—GREG J. DUNCAN

Acknowledgments

Many minds and hands, over many years, have made this monograph possible. There is truly a cast of thousands, because, without respondent and interviewer cooperation, we would have little data. The material presented in this monograph is an edited compilation of numerous documents written by the PSID staff over the course of the study and most especially in the last 10 years. I am greatly indebted to the following individuals who were authors of those original documents: Drs. Greg Duncan, Daniel Hill, Charles Brown, and James Lepkowski; Deborah Laren, Tecla Loup, Barbara Browne, Marita Servais, Mary Wreford, and Wei-Jun Jean Yeung.

The discussion about weighting and sampling error calculations owes a great deal to Drs. James Lepkowski, Daniel Hill, and Greg Duncan. The information about literature based on the PSID has benefited substantially from Dr. Charles Brown's and Wei-Jun Jean Yeung's vigilant tracking of the literature. The analysis examples reflect the skillful and careful work of Deborah Laren and Wei-Jun Jean Yeung.

Considerable debt is also owed to PSID, SRC, and ICPSR staff members subjected to numerous technical questions about study procedures; these patient people include Ronald Amos, Bonnie Bittman, Barbara Browne, Heather Hewett, Margaret Hoad, Tecla Loup, Thomas Gonzales, Marita Servais, Charles Stallman, and Janet Vavra. A number of PSID staff members are valuable storehouses of important details about the study. Tecla Loup, especially, has become a living resource of PSID lore, past and present.

The monograph has benefited directly from the efforts and suggestions of several people. Considerable debt is owed to Drs. Peter Marsden, Annemette Sorensen, Greg Duncan, James Lepkowski, Daniel Kasprzyk, and Patricia Smith; Terry Adams, Joan Brinser, Barbara Browne, Dorothy Duncan, Deborah Laren,

Tecla Loup, and Wei-Jun Jean Yeung. Their helpful suggestions, diligence, and care have increased the reliability and clarity of the monograph.

Debts are owed as well to current and former PSID staff members who built the PSID over the years. The major persons, of course, are Dr. James N. Morgan, the founding father of the study, who continues to inspire and nurture it even after official retirement, and Dr. Greg J. Duncan, at the helm and steadfastly steering the study through calm and turbulent seas. Other persons include Drs. Nancy Baerwaldt, Jacob Benus, Richard Coe, Mary Corcoran, Linda Datcher-Loury, Jonathan Dickinson, Katherine Dickinson, Daniel Hill, Saul Hoffman, John Holmes, and Jim Smith; Anita Ernst, Beverly Harris, Priscilla Hildebrandt, Wanda Lemon, Anne Sears, and Kathryn Terrazas. And contributions to the study have been made by the NSF Board of Overseers, which has comprised over the years a long and highly distinguished list of scholars.

1. Introduction

Monograph Purpose and Content

This monograph describes the origins, design, procedures, and broad analytical potential of one of the major data bases in the social sciences—the Panel Study of Income Dynamics (PSID). After a brief review of the PSID's background, the monograph discusses the major design parameters, field procedures, and data preparation activities. These chapters describe the data collection process and serve as important background for understanding how PSID data come into being and what they represent. Issues of the quality of PSID data are addressed next, with reporting of evidence about a number of different quality dimensions. The remainder of the monograph delves into the data themselves—what topics are covered, what data files are available—with crucial information regarding analysis issues, key variables, and choice of data files. Chapter 8, "Data Analysis," provides details of several analysis examples so that the reader can see the assembly of parts needed to create estimates of earnings regressions, long-run poverty status, changes in women's income following divorce, and correlations between parents' income and a child's adult income.

The monograph takes the reader from the drawing board to a completed product with a minimum of detail. Where most applicable, it notes other PSID documents, such as the PSID's documentation books and *User Guide*, that can provide further details about particular aspects of the study. In the final chapter, information is provided about obtaining these documents and the data files themselves. Throughout the monograph, italics are used to distinguish terms with special meaning in the context of the PSID, and full capital letters are used to designate PSID variable names.

Overview of the PSID

The Panel Study of Income Dynamics (PSID) is a longitudinal survey of a representative sample of U.S. individuals (men, women, and children) and the families in which they reside. It has been ongoing since 1968. Data are collected annually, and the data files contain the full span of information collected over the course of the study. PSID data can be used for cross-sectional, longitudinal, and intergenerational analyses and for studying both individuals and families. The study emphasizes the dynamic aspects of economic and demographic behavior, but it contains a wide range of measures, including sociological and psychological ones. Between 1968 and 1988, the PSID collected information regarding approximately 37,500 individuals and spanning as much as 21 years of their lives.

The general design and core content of the study have remained largely unchanged, and considerable effort has been expended to clean the data. These two features greatly enhance the PSID's potential for longitudinal analysis. Preparation and distribution of comprehensive documentation and the *User Guide* (Survey Research Center, 1984) also facilitate use of the PSID data.

The study has been conducted at the Survey Research Center, Institute for Social Research, University of Michigan, with the Inter-University Consortium for Political and Social Research (ICPSR) data archive handling the public distribution of the data files, documentation, and *User Guide*. PSID data files have been disseminated widely throughout the United States and to numerous foreign countries.

Starting with a national sample of approximately 4,800 U.S. households in 1968, the PSID has traced individuals from those households since that time, whether or not they are living in the same dwelling or with the same people. Adults have been followed as they have grown older, and children have been observed as they advance through childhood and into adulthood, forming families of their own. Each year, information is collected about the PSID's *sample members* (members of the PSID's 1968 sample families or their offspring) and their current coresidents (spouses, cohabitors, children, and others living with them), even if those coresidents were not part of original-sample families.

Because the original focus of the study was the dynamics of poverty, the 1968 sample included a disproportionately large number of low-income households. The oversampling of families poor in the late 1960s resulted in a sizable subsample of blacks. Probability-of-selection weights enable analysts to make estimates from the sample that are representative of the U.S. population. In the absence of nonresponse bias, the PSID's rules for tracking individuals and families over time lead to accurate representation of the nonimmigrant U.S. population both cross-sectionally each year and in terms of change since 1968. To help correct for omissions in representing post-1968 immigrants, a representative sample of 2,043 Latino (Mexican, Cuban, and Puerto Rican) households was added in 1990.

The study's tracking rules, along with its Latino subsample addition in 1990, have meant substantial increases in the number of individuals in the study as it has progressed through time. In 1968, the PSID gathered information about approximately 18,000 individuals; by 1988, this number had grown to a cumulative total of about 37,500. Similarly, the number of family units has increased from just under 5,000 at the beginning of the study to about 7,000 currently, not including Latino households.

The PSID provides a wide variety of information at the family and individual levels as well as some information about the locations in which sample households reside. The central focus of the data is economic and demographic, with substantial detail on income sources and amounts, employment, family composition changes, and residential location. Content of a more sociological or psychological nature is also included in some waves of the study. Information gathered in the survey applies to the circumstances of the family unit as a whole (e.g., type of housing) and to particular persons in the family unit (e.g., age, earnings). Some data are collected about all individuals in the family unit, but the most extensive data are gathered for the family head (who is male in married-couple families but female or male otherwise) and wife. Information about the study's core topics (e.g., income, employment, family composition) is gathered annually, and this is supplemented with data on additional topics (e.g., health, wealth, retirement plans, flows of time and money help among families and their friends, and motivation and efficacy) gathered intermittently. The amount and variety of data are substantial; over 300 pages are required to list, by topic and wave, the variables on the study's main, cross-year data file.

The PSID staff merges each new wave of data with prior waves to provide comprehensive coverage of information collected for individuals and families during the entire course of the study. These multiwave data files become publicly available upon completion of the merging, numerous data-quality checks, and generation of variables. This usually occurs 18-24 months following the completion of interviewing.

Origin of the PSID

As part of Lyndon Johnson's War on Poverty, the Office of Economic Opportunity (OEO) directed the U.S. Bureau of the Census to conduct a nationwide assessment of the extent to which the War on Poverty was affecting people's economic well-being. This census study, called the Survey of Economic Opportunity (SEO), completed interviews with about 30,000 households, first in 1966 and again in 1967.

Interest in continuing this national study of economic well-being led OEO to approach the Survey Research Center (SRC) at the University of Michigan about interviewing a subsample of approximately 2,000 low-income SEO households. Professor James N. Morgan, who became the new study's director at SRC, argued successfully for adding a fresh cross section of households from the SRC national sampling frame so that the new study would be representative of the entire population of the United States, including nonpoor as well as poor households. It was also decided to follow, and keep as part of the sample, members of the families who moved away from their original households to set up new households, such as children who came of age during the study. In this way, the sample could remain representative of the nation's families and individuals over time.

The study came to be known as the Panel Study of Income Dynamics. It began interviewing in 1968, successfully completing interviews with 4,802 households across 40 states—1,872 low-income households from the SEO plus 2,930 households drawn from the SRC national sampling frame. The year 1991 marked the study's 24th annual wave of interviewing, with its family units having substantially increased in number and having spread to cover all 50 states as well as some other countries.

Administration and Funding

The PSID has been funded principally by a collection of federal agencies, including the Office of Economic Opportunity; the Assistant Secretary for Planning and Evaluation of the Department of Health, Education and Welfare (now Health and Human Services); the Departments of Labor and Agriculture; the National Science Foundation; the National Institute of Child Health and Human Development (NICHD); and the National Institute on Aging (NIA). The Ford, Sloan, and Rockefeller foundations have provided important supplementary grants to the PSID. Since 1983, the National Science Foundation (NSF) has been the principal sponsor of the study, with substantial continuing support from the Office of the Assistant Secretary for Planning and Evaluation (ASPE) of the Department of Health and Human Services. Since 1982, the study has had an advisory Board of Overseers, created by the NSF to foster input from the national community of scholars, researchers, and policymakers.

From its beginning in 1968 until 1989, the PSID was directed at the Survey Research Center, University of Michigan by James N. Morgan, now emeritus. From 1982 through 1989 responsibility for running the study was also shared by Greg J. Duncan (as co-director), Daniel H. Hill, and Martha S. Hill. Since 1989 Greg Duncan has directed the study, with Martha Hill and James N. Lepkowski as co-directors.

Illustrative Uses of the PSID

Two key features give the PSID its unique analytic power: (a) individuals are followed over very long time periods and in the context of their family setting and (b) families are tracked across generations, with interviews often conducted simultaneously with multiple generations of the same families. The type of information the study collects, in conjunction with these unique qualities, builds a number of strengths, including the following:

• continuous representation of families and of individuals of all ages;
• long annual—and, in some cases, monthly—time series of employment, income, and demographic information, reported through annual interviews;

- extensive intergenerational information, with a long time series of adulthood information obtained from each generation directly, information after individuals have become adults as well as during their childhoods, and comparable detail for all children from the same families;
- coverage of diverse supplemental topics (e.g., health, wealth, saving, kinship);
- recent additions of information, accessible to data users under special circumstances, about neighborhoods (e.g., census tract) and about health and mortality (e.g., from Medicare records and the National Death Index); and
- extensive longitudinal, as well as cross-sectional, checking of the data and comprehensive documentation of the full data set since its start in 1968.

These features make the PSID one of the most widely used and influential data sets in the social science research community. Some 200 institutions have requested copies of PSID data. And over 700 publications using PSID data have appeared in economic, demographic, and sociological journals and books. The data are also extensively used for dissertations, reports, conference presentations, and working papers. A comprehensive bibliography is available from PSID staff upon request (see the final section of this monograph).

Areas of basic economic research addressed with the data include labor supply, consumption, life cycle earnings, male-female and black-white wage differences, unions, compensating wage differentials, dynamic aspects of income distribution, income transfer programs, savings and wealth, unpaid productive activities, taxes, and various methodological studies. PSID topics of interest to researchers in several disciplines—demographers, sociologists, psychologists, and economists—include poverty and welfare experiences during adulthood or childhood, motivation and economic mobility, changes in family structure (e.g., births, divorce, remarriage), child support, kinship networks, out-of-wedlock births, teenage childbearing, and the intergenerational transmission of economic status. This diversity of topics reflects the philosophy of the PSID to ask limited sets of questions about a wide variety of topics rather than extensive questions about only a few topics. The study's multifaceted information is couched in the context of substantial detail about income, employment, and family composition.

A short listing of topics can only begin to provide a flavor for the PSID's analysis possibilities. The data offer vast opportunities for research. The data are also complex, and it is important to have a clear understanding of a number of features of the study to make correct use of them. This monograph provides analysis examples to help a potential data user see important steps involved in analyzing PSID data. Before presenting those examples, though, the monograph describes a number of important features of the study.

2. Study Design

Overall Design

The PSID gathers information about families and all individuals in those families through its annual interviews.[1] A single primary adult—usually the male adult *head*,[2] if there is one—serves as the sole respondent. Sometimes the *wife* (or cohabitor, referred to as *"wife"*) of the head agrees to grant an interview when the *head* does not. The single household respondent provides information about him- or herself and about all other *family members*.[3]

The study's original households constitute a national probability sample of U.S. households as of 1967. Its rules for following household members were designed to maintain a representative sample of families at any point in time as well as across time. To accomplish this, the PSID tracks members of its wave 1 (1968) families, including all those leaving to establish separate family units. Children born to an *original-sample member* are classified as *sample members* and are eligible for tracking as separate family units when they set up their own households. Ex-spouses and other adult *sample members* who move out of PSID family units are tracked to their new family units. This procedure replicates the population's family-building activity and produces a dynamic sample of families each year. New PSID families form when children grow up and establish separate households or when marriage partners go separate ways. This results in growth over time in both the number of family units and the number of people residing with a *sample member* at some time during the study.

Information is gathered about all persons residing in the family unit, but, in most waves, there is only one respondent per family unit (usually the *head*). The most detailed information is collected each year about the *heads* of family units. Since the late 1970s, however, the PSID has sought to collect the same detailed information for *wives/"wives"* (by *"wives,"* we mean cohabitors) as for *heads*. For special supplements gathering retrospective history information in 1976 and 1985, the study conducted separate interviews with all *wives/"wives"* of *heads* as well as their husbands. Except for the very early years of the study, cohabitors have been treated in a similar manner to husbands and wives.

The general design of the study has remained largely unchanged over time; however, the mode of interviewing has changed. From 1968 through 1972, the PSID conducted in-person interviews. In 1973, to reduce costs, the study began doing the majority of interviews by telephone. Since that time, in-person interviews have been conducted only with respondents who do not have telephones (roughly 500 each year) or who have special circumstances that make a telephone interview unfeasible. To further reduce costs, and because long interviews are difficult by telephone, interview length was also reduced in 1973. The interview averaged about one hour when it was conducted in person; since the change to telephone interviewing, the length has averaged 20 to 30 minutes.

As discussed in Chapter 6, "Content," the PSID has maintained a core of questions addressing issues relevant to income dynamics and demographic change. In addition to the central core, there have been a number of supplements to the core, adding questions on a wide variety of other topics. These supplements have led to the creation and release of a number of special files that complement the main PSID data files.

Sample Design

Sample frame. The initial sample for the PSID actually consisted of two independent samples: a cross-sectional, national sample (based on stratified multistage selection of the civilian noninstitutional population of the United States) and a national sample of low-income families.[4] The cross-section sample was drawn by the Survey Research Center (SRC). Commonly called the *SRC sample*, it was an equal probability sample of households in the 48 coterminous states designed to yield about 3,000 completed interviews. (In fact, 2,930 interviews were made in 1968 from this sample.)

The second sample of responding PSID families, known as the *SEO sample*, came from the Survey of Economic Opportunity (SEO), conducted by the Bureau of the Census for the Office of Economic Opportunity. The PSID selected from the SEO's sample, the goal being to obtain about 2,000 low-income families with *heads* under 60 years old. In fact, 1,872 families were successfully interviewed. The *SEO sample* was confined to standard metropolitan statistical areas (SMSAs) and to non-SMSAs in the southern region, and it involves unequal selection probabilities.

Both the *SRC* and the *SEO* were subject to nonresponse in the first wave (1968). Three factors played a special role in preventing successful interviews with the *SEO sample*:

(1) There was nonresponse in the original census survey from which the *SEO sample* was selected.
(2) Sampled census respondents were asked by the Bureau of the Census to sign a release to allow their names to be passed on to the SRC. Approximately one quarter of the households failed to sign the release.
(3) The OEO failed to transmit some sampled addresses to SRC.

The PSID sample combines the *SRC* and *SEO samples*. Both samples are probability samples (i.e., samples for which every element in the population has a known nonzero chance of selection). Their combination is also a probability sample. The combination, however, is a sample with unequal selection probabilities, and, as a result, compensatory weighting is needed in estimation, at least for descriptive statistics. (The various disciplines disagree about the need for weighting in model-based estimation.) Weight adjustments are also needed to attempt to compensate for differential nonresponse in 1968 and subsequent waves. As explained in Chapter 8, "Data Analysis," and detailed in the PSID's technical documentation, weights supplied on PSID data files are designed to compensate for both unequal selection probabilities and differential attrition.

Latino supplemental sample. The original PSID sample contains too few Latino households to provide reliable estimates either for Latinos as a group or for major subgroups of Latinos. In addition, Latinos entering the United States since 1968 are not represented in the basic PSID sample unless they coreside with persons in the United States in 1968. To help reduce these shortfalls, a sample of 2,043 Latino households was interviewed and added to the PSID sample beginning in the 1990 wave. Funding for this supplemental sample came from the Ford Foundation, the Rockefeller Foundation, the ASPE in the Department of Health and Human Services, the Employment Training Administration in the Department of Labor, and the NSF.

The 1990 addition of a *Latino sample* is designed to provide precisely the kind of representative information about Latinos that is now available for blacks and non-Latino whites in the original PSID. The sample was originally selected for the Latino National Political Survey (LNPS), a 1989 study of the political participation of Latino households cosponsored by the Inter-University Program for Latino Research and administered by the Center for Mexican American Studies of the University of Texas at Austin. The LNPS did not attempt to cover the entire Latino population in the United States. However, it covered at least 89% of the three largest Latino subgroups—the Mexican-, Puerto Rican-, and Cuban-origin populations.

Latino sample members were asked extensive background information in their initial interview in 1990, including marital and fertility histories. In addition, questions were added to the 1990 interview to enable calculation of selection probability weights so that the Latino sample can be combined with the existing PSID sample for analysis purposes. The PSID plans to continue gathering comparable information from the *Latino* and *original PSID samples* and to combine the two samples in PSID data files.

Tracking rules. The PSID's tracking rules call for following members of the original family units and their adult offspring to whatever living arrangements they experience. Information is gathered about these *sample members* and their coresidents if they are living in a household (i.e., noninstitutional) situation. A *family member* who moves out of a PSID family is eligible for interviewing as a separate family unit if he or she is a *sample member and* he or she is

18 years old or older *and* living in a different, independent household.[5] If a *sample member* 18 or older moves to an institution such as a prison, a college dormitory, or the military, the PSID records this fact and attaches an *institutional status* data record to the family he or she left. The PSID keeps track of the location of *sample members* living in institutional housing. Interviews are attempted with them if and when they leave the institution to set up their own households.

Notes

1. A PSID family is defined somewhat differently than a Bureau of the Census family. The differences are described in the "Unit of Analysis" section in Chapter 8.
2. In a married-couple family, the PSID defines *head* of a family as the husband, unless the husband is severely disabled. This definition was adopted from the Bureau of the Census in 1968, and, although dated, it has been maintained for the sake of consistency and ease of following panel members.
3. Individuals are classified as PSID *family members* if, at the time of interview, they are either residing in an interviewed family unit (and not temporary roommates, roomers, or visiting friends or relatives) or temporarily away from an interviewed family unit and in an institution (e.g., college, jail, hospital, the military).
4. PSID *sample members* also include some persons in institutions in 1968. Children and stepchildren aged 25 or younger in 1968 and living in institutions (e.g., in military barracks or college dormitories) but attached to families interviewed by the PSID that year were classified as *sample members*. They have been interviewed after leaving the institutions and forming their own households.
5. Under certain circumstances, the PSID follows sample members under age 18 who have set up their own households. For example, a 16-year-old daughter who gets married and lives in a household other than her parents' will be followed by the PSID.

3. Field Procedures

Data Collection

The PSID data are collected by the national interviewing staff of the Survey Research Center (SRC) at the University of Michigan.

The SRC interviewing staff is supported by supervisors, the SRC Field Office administrative and clerical staff, and the PSID staff.

Activities for a given wave of data collection begin with preparation of field instruments. The primary instruments include the questionnaire (a document approximately 100 pages in length in recent years), cover sheets (which record confidential information such as names and relationships of *family members* and persons to contact in case we have difficulty locating the family), and an interviewer instruction manual (approximately 400 pages long in recent years). The PSID staff, with advice from the Board of Overseers, updates and revises these instruments annually.

PSID data collection for a given wave extends from March through September using a national field staff of interviewers and supervisors dispersed across the United States but coordinated by SRC Field Office personnel in Ann Arbor. Approximately 115 interviewers and 6 to 12 supervisors (not including those for the *Latino subsample*) work on the PSID each year. Field supervisors hire and train new interviewers, monitor interviewer productivity and quality, check completeness and accuracy of interviews, and help solve problems that arise for interviewers or respondents. The SRC Field Office coordinates production interviewing by preparing supervisor and interviewer sample assignments, responding to interviewer and supervisor questions, and distributing interviewing materials to and collecting them from interviewers and supervisors. The SRC Field Office maintains a sample control and inventory system for logging interviews and cover sheets on a daily basis as they are received from interviewers and supervisors.

The PSID staff assists with recruiting, hiring, and training of new interviewers. They also answer questions from the Field Office about locating and interviewing respondents, and they help in conducting pretest telephone interviews. In addition, they travel to training conferences, communicate with interviewers and supervisors as necessary, and monitor reports from the Field Office sample control and inventory system.

Interviewer hiring and training. The total number of new interviewers hired varies from year to year. Prior to data collection, the SRC Field Office and supervisors determine how many interviewers on the existing staff are available for the coming round of data collection. Additional interviewers are recruited in locations where sample cases are located. The SRC Field Office hires new interviewers and arranges for basic interviewer training by supervisors. All interviewers, both newly hired and continuing staff, attend prestudy conferences arranged by the SRC Field Office prior to the start of data collection.

Monitoring. A proportion of each interviewer's completed cases are recontacted by supervisors to verify that the interview took place. The proportion varies from approximately 5% of the completed interviews taken by experienced interviewers to 10% for new interviewers. Verification consists of contacting respondents and asking them approximately 10 questions, including how well the interviewer conducted the interview, how long it took, and several questions from various parts of the PSID questionnaire.

Assignment of interviewers to respondents. The 1968 PSID sample was clustered into more than 200 primary sampling areas for the convenience of data collection administration and reduction of costs. Since that time, PSID *sample members* have moved to new locations, and the sample has dispersed throughout all 50 states in the United States and several foreign countries. In each wave, the PSID interviews one member (usually the *head*) of each of its prior year families. The study also initiates interviewing with a yearly average of about 250 *new heads* (*sample* children who have established their own households, spouses of these sample children, or formerly married persons who have established new, separate households).

Approximately 92% of the sample are interviewed by telephone each year, with interviewers conducting interviews from their own homes. The remaining 8% of the sample (25% of the *Latino subsample*) are respondents who must be interviewed in person because they have (a) no telephone or (b) hearing or health problems or other personal circumstances that require in-person contact. In the early years of the study, assignments of interviewers to respondents were made on the basis of geographic proximity. Assignments for in-person interviews continue to be made this way. However, in 1985, the PSID sample for telephone interviewing was redistributed across interviewers so as to minimize long-distance telephone charges. Because of telephone rate structures, this increased the proportion of out-of-state relative to in-state long-distance interviews, shifting long-distance respondents away from their prior wave interviewers. Prior to 1985 and since the redistribution in 1985, respondents have been assigned their prior wave interviewer whenever possible. The PSID is converting to a computer-assisted interviewing system during the three-year period from 1991 to 1993. The initial step is to centralize the interviewing as much as possible at the SRC telephone facility in Ann Arbor. A transition away from paper-and-pencil interviewing and to a computer-assisted telephone interviewing (CATI) and computer-assisted personal interviewing (CAPI) system will then begin.

Maximizing Response Rates

In a panel survey such as the PSID, maintaining a high reinterview response rate from one wave to the next is crucial. Given the mobility of the U.S. population, and the difficulty of retaining respondent cooperation, considerable effort is required to maintain high levels of follow-up cooperation.

The PSID's field period is quite lengthy (running from March through September) to allow for tracking of *sample members* who have moved and persuasion of reluctant ones. Additional PSID strategies for maintaining high response rates include the following: (a) payments to respondents for the interview and for returning a change-of-address postcard (currently $15 for the interview and $5 for the postcard); (b) annual preparation and mailing of a booklet to respondents summarizing how PSID data are being analyzed and used in policy debates; (c) personalized persuasion letters for persons reluctant to continue as respondents; (d) requests, at the end of each interview, for the names and telephone numbers of friends or relatives who would know the respondent's location if he or she were to move; (e) a staff person with ready access to this information who helps interviewers "troubleshoot" difficult cases; (f) continuity of interviewer-respondent matches; (g) allowing personal interviews in situations where telephone interviewing is problematic; and (h) periodic mailings by first-class mail (checks, respondent reports, announcement of the upcoming interview), spaced throughout the period between interviews, that produce changes of address for respondents who move.

4. Data Preparation

Coding and Cleaning

The PSID minimizes the use of interviewers as coders but encourages them to make extensive marginal notes in the questionnaire when complicated situations arise. Editing and coding of the data are done after the interview is turned in to Ann Arbor staff, who have access to prior waves of information. Extensive effort is devoted to assuring data quality, including hand editing of variables of major importance to the study's overall purpose and the assignment of values to missing items based on past as well as current information. (Variables with imputations are flagged as such.) Numerous within-wave and between-wave consistency checks are also made in the course of data processing.

Precoding editing. The PSID puts the interview information through a twofold editing system (demographic editing and economic editing) before data are entered in machine-readable format. This editing system detects and corrects many errors before the data are released to the public.

Demographic editing is done to ensure correct identification of people in the study and to ensure that the appropriate questions have been asked about each person. These activities are crucial for accurately tracking individuals through time and charting their relationships and demographic events. Data collection is complicated by the family focus of the study and the substantial probability of change in family composition from one year to the next. It is impossible to know in advance exactly who will be present in any given family when an interview is made. Both the designation of the appropriate respondent and the flow of the questionnaire are very sensitive to family structure.

Family composition change can also affect who serves as respondent and thus what parts of the questionnaire are relevant to the family. A series of checks help ensure that the correct individuals have been tracked and interviewed when families experience marriages, divorces, and other important changes. Each interview is thoroughly checked to make sure the appropriate questions have been asked about each person and to assure that family composition is treated in a consistent manner throughout the interview. Any errors or omissions in the interview are noted, and decisions are made about whether the problems are serious enough to necessitate recontacting the respondent for resolution.

Because economic change is a major focus of the PSID, the economic data receive special attention in precoding editing. The purpose of economic editing is to ensure the accuracy and integrity of the economic data. For each wave, economic editors apply decision rules and judgments to some 300 key income, employment, housing cost, and family expenditure variables. Employment situations and means of compensation, housing and home financing, employment and nonemployment spells, income sources and receipts, and food expenditures are all interpreted in the editing process within the context of study concepts and procedures.

Editing of income amounts takes the family unit and recent changes in its composition into account. Income amounts for people moving into and out of the family are edited to reflect only those portions earned or received while the person was part of the family. Further, because economic family units and biologic families must be distinguished, editors must often deal with transfers of money and shared expenditures within the same "family" or between families when more than one family lives in the same household.

Editing involves a large number of checks for internal consistency and, where necessary, imputations or adjustments using standard procedures and previous years' data. Any interview with significant missing information or inconsistencies may be returned to the field for clarification or correction.

Coding. Once the demographic and economic editing are completed, coding operations begin. Two separate activities occur here: assignment of occupation and industry codes and data entry of the questionnaire information.

Data entry is performed by the SRC Coding Section using SRC's Direct Data Entry (DDE) computer coding system. Data entry of PSID data is similar to coding procedures followed on conventional, cross-sectional surveys. Handwritten information on the interviews is converted to machine-readable form, and consistency and wild-code checks are performed automatically.

Postcoding cleaning. When the raw data files are received from the Coding Section, current family- and individual-level data are separated. Separate processing procedures are implemented for each level of data simultaneously, with feedback and corrections being made between the two files throughout the data cleaning phase. Initially, the data file is checked for missing or twice-coded cases. Then, comparisons on selected data items are made between the current and the previous wave. The current wave individual data are merged and checked against previous waves. It is essential that each of the more than 37,000 individuals be accounted for and that his or her data be associated with only one current wave family.

The cross-wave checking must be completed in time to generate materials needed for the following wave's interview. These checks ensure that all persons in the current wave family match persons in the previous wave family, both with regard to unique individual identifiers and with regard to gender, age, and relationship to the *head* of the family unit. Further, the family-level data for current and previous waves are compared for consistency in state and county coding, housing status and mobility, agreement between ages of *head* and *wife/ "wife,"* changes in family size, and marital status.

Computer-Generated Variables

Each wave's data contain about 100 family-level and 50 individual-level variables that are not directly asked of respondents but are computer generated from measures obtained in the interview or from previous waves' data. At the family level, generated variables include federal income tax liability and marginal tax rates of each tax unit within the family; sampling information such as sampling weight and sampling error computation unit; location measures such as region, state and county FIPS (U.S. Federal Information Processing Standards) code, and employment conditions in county; and various summary measures intended to relieve analysts of the burdens of constructing variables such as total number of children of various ages, poverty thresholds, income deciles, and marital status change measures. Individual-level generated variables include updated marital and fertility histories, demographic information on and unique identifiers of parents, attrition/institutional status, and the individual weight.

After the generated variables are constructed and added to the data file, a final check is made between current wave family and individual data to ensure detection of any errors introduced in the generated variable or data cleaning operations. This final check is made just before the data are turned over to the Inter-University Consortium for Political and Social Research (ICPSR) for public release, generally two years after data cleaning began.

Missing-Data Conventions

About 80 of the PSID's variables that appear wave after wave are assigned an imputed value when there is missing data. These variables are mostly income and work hour measures. As an example of the imputation process, say that the interview contains no report of prior calendar-year income from wages and salaries for the *head* but does indicate that she has the same work position as the last year and contains a report of current salary. Editors are instructed to impute a value on income from wages and salaries equal to the current salary. Under some circumstances, the interview will be sent back to interviewers to reask for the missing information rather than try to impute it. The variables for which the PSID imputes missing data have no missing-data codes; instead, a companion accuracy-code variable is constructed to indicate whether, in a given record, data were imputed and, if so, how close to a real value the imputed one is likely to be (an assessment of the margin of error based largely on how much case-specific information was available for making an assignment).

Most PSID variables have missing-data codes, but no one value is always designated as a missing-data value. The most common missing-data code in PSID data is a full field of 9s, indicating that a response should have been obtained but the information was "not ascertained" (NA).[1] A full field of 9s, however, does not always indicate missing data; a full field of 9s in an imputed variable (a variable that has a companion accuracy-code variable registering the likely reliability of the imputation) indicates an "over-the-field" value—a value larger than the number of columns allocated for the variable (e.g., 99999 indicating that the value was greater than or equal to $99,999 in a five column income variable). Zero codes also have various meanings in the PSID; hence the study does not designate zero as a missing-data value. A zero code can mean a substantive "None" value, such as no taxable income as the real value for the variable TOTAL TAXABLE INCOME. Or a zero code can mean "inappropriate, question not asked." This is assigned, for example, to nonmovers for the variable based on the question "Why did you (*head*) move?" Users should take careful note of this when they wish to designate zero as a missing-data code.

Construction of Weights

As explained in Chapter 2, "Study Design," the PSID sample combines the *SRC* and *SEO samples*. Both samples are probability samples, thus so is their combination. The combination is, however, a sample with unequal selection probabilities. Compensatory weights are calculated to enable the analyst to derive national estimates from the PSID sample. The weights adjust for differential attrition as well as selection probabilities, but it is the selection probabilities that by far determine the largest portion of the variation in weight values.

The 1968 weights. The first step in developing weights is to determine the inclusion probabilities for each component sample separately in the 1968 wave. This is straightforward in the case of the *SRC sample*. Sampled families were selected with equal probability (approximately 1 in 15,300 to obtain the desired sample size). Because all members of sampled families were included in the sample, this probability applies also to *sample members*. An analysis of response rates by region and type of area (self-representing areas divided into central cities and suburbs, non-self-representing areas divided into SMSAs and non-SMSAs) showed appreciable variation across the 16 cells, ranging from a response rate of 60% in central cities in the north-central region to 87% in non-SMSAs in the South. Making the assumption that non-responding families were missing at random within each cell, the probability of family j being included in the *SRC sample* is thus

PR_j, where R_j is the response rate for the family's nonresponse adjustment cell.

In the case of the *SEO sample,* the inclusion probability of a low-income family with *head* under age 60 living in an SMSA or a non-SMSA in the South depended on the following factors:

- the inclusion probability for the census sample (p_j for family j)
- the subsample selection probability for the PSID's *SEO sample* (q_j)
- the receiving rate of sampled addresses by SRC (t_j)
- the response rate achieved by SRC (r_j)

The inclusion and subsample selection probabilities were known for each person in the *SEO sample.* The receiving rate for a sampled family was the rate at which addresses were received in their primary sampling unit (PSU) or group of PSUs, computed separately for white and nonwhite families. The response rate for a sampled family was the response rate within a cell formed according to geographic region (four levels), self-representing or non-self-representing areas within region, and non-self-representing areas divided into SMSAs and non-SMSAs in the South. The underlying assumptions are that nonresponse is random within family types within PSUs and that nonresponding families are missing at random within cells. The overall inclusion probability of a family in the SEO sample is thus p_jq_j. This rate is further adjusted by the receiving and response rates, t_jr_j.

To develop the weights for this combined sample, the overall inclusion probability for being in either the *SRC* or the *SEO sample* was determined for each sampled family. This inclusion probability for any given family is the sum of the probabilities of being included in the *SRC* and *SEO samples.* Strictly speaking, this sum is the expected number of appearances in the sample. However, given that the probability of being selected for both samples is negligible, the expected number and the inclusion probability are approximately equal.

To determine the inclusion probabilities, we divided the combined sample into three parts: (a) the *SEO sample,* (b) the low-income families in the *SRC sample* from SMSAs and from non-SMSAs in the South, and (c) the rest of the *SRC sample.* Families in the first and second parts have a chance of being selected for both the *SRC* and the *SEO samples.* Their probabilities of inclusion are approximately $P(j) = PR_j + p_jq_jt_jr_j$. Families in the third part can enter the combined sample only through the *SRC sample*. Their inclusion probabilities are simply $P(j) = PR_j$. The weights are then made inversely proportional to the $P(j)$; in fact, the weights are set equal to $(400P[j])^{-1}$.

To compute $P(j)$ for families in the first and second parts, it is necessary to know the inclusion probability both for the sample in which the family was selected and for the other sample. It is easy to determine the *SRC* inclusion probabilities for *SEO sample* families. However, determining *SEO* inclusion probabilities for low-income *SRC sample* families in SMSAs and non-SMSAs in the South requires estimates of p_j and t_j. Estimation of p_j and t_j for *SRC sample* families in this special group requires further assumptions, which are detailed in the study's technical documentation.

Adjustments to the sampling rates and family weights since 1968. Panel studies of families like the PSID must cope with the dynamic aspects of the population of families. New families are established or "born" into the population when children leave their parental homes, when married couples split into different families through separation or divorce, or in cases of immigration. If a panel study is to maintain a representative sample of both the individuals and the families in the population, then there must be a replacement mechanism that allows new families and individuals to enter the sample with known selection probabilities.

The PSID began in 1968 with a probability sample of families. Because all 1968 family members were considered *sample members*, the sampling probability that applies to the family also applies to each member of that family. In the first year of the study, then, the family weight is the appropriate individual weight for all individuals in that family.

Over time, individuals retain their selection probabilities, with possible adjustments for individual attrition. Individuals enter the population through birth and immigration. The PSID replacement mechanism for births is to include individuals born into *sample families* as part of the sample of individuals, assigning to them the selection probability and weight of the family into which they are born. The PSID has no complete mechanism for adding immigrants. The sample of 2,043 Latino households, drawn by Temple University's Institute for Survey Research in

1988 and first interviewed as part of the PSID in 1990, is the only attempt that has been made to make the PSID representative with respect to immigration since 1968.

The "birth" and "death" of families is a more complicated process to account for in the study design. If a married couple that is part of the original sample breaks up into two families through divorce, *and neither remarries*, then each new family has the selection probability of the family prior to the divorce. The two new families have the same weight as the original family, and weighted estimates from the sample reflect the fact that there are now two of these families in the population as a result of these kinds of changes.

However, a new family can be "born" when a divorced *sample* spouse marries a *nonsample* individual or when a child in a *sample* family leaves home and marries a *nonsample* person. The PSID follows all such families. The new family has two ways of being selected, either through the *sample* spouse or through the *nonsample* spouse. The selection probability of the *sample* spouse is known, but that of the *nonsample* spouse is not known. The PSID assumes that people marry others like themselves—that is, with the same selection probability.[2] Under this assumption, the selection probability of the new family is twice the selection probability of the *sample* spouse, and the family weight is, therefore, half of the individual weight of the *sample* spouse. Children born into these families are assigned this halved weight as their individual weight.

When the family contains two *sample* adults, typically the adults are both *original sample members* with the same weight. They were selected as a family in the 1968 sample. However, there are a few instances in which *sample members* from two different 1968 families have married. Their individual weights are the same as their original 1968 family weights; their new family weight is computed as the average of their two individual weights.

In summary, rules for family weights in the PSID are as follows:

- If the family contains two married adults, both of whom are *sample members*, then the family weight is the average of the two individual weights.
- If the family is headed by a single adult, then that person's individual selection probability and weight also apply to the family.
- If the family contains two married adults, one of whom is a *sample member* while the other is not, then it is assumed that the selection probability for the *nonsample* spouse equals the selection probability of the *sample*

spouse. The selection probability of the family is taken to be twice that of the *sample* spouse and the family weight is taken to be half the individual weight of the *sample* spouse.

These procedures have important implications for the analyst who wishes to make estimates of population parameters from the sample. The decision to follow all sample individuals as they form new households means that the unweighted proportion of young families in the sample is larger than the proportion of young families in the population as a whole. This large proportion of young families is not a consequence of the PSID's decision to combine a cross-section sample with a low-income subsample; it results from trying to track all sample children to their adult locations. Analysts who restrict their attention to the cross-section part of the sample will observe this as well. The disproportionate numbers across subgroups of different ages present no problems if weights are used.

Adjustments to individual weights since 1968. The preceding paragraphs have been concerned principally with the probabilities of entire families falling into the PSID sample. Many of the more interesting questions that can be addressed with the PSID data have to do with individuals. The probability that a given individual was selected for the sample in 1968 is exactly the same as the probability of selection of the family in which the individual was living (or the parental family to which children or stepchildren under age 25 and in institutions in 1968 were attached) at that time. Unlike the family sampling rates, individual sampling rates are not affected by subsequent family composition changes. Adjustments are made to individual sampling rates for attrition subsequent to 1968. Individuals who are members of groups with high attrition rates have their effective sampling rates reduced and their weights increased relative to individuals in groups with low attrition. These attrition adjustments are detailed in *A Panel Study of Income Dynamics: Procedures and Tape Codes 1984 Interviewing Year, Wave XVII* (Survey Research Center, 1986, pp. 66-76). The attrition adjustments are a small component of the weights because differential attrition in the PSID is small. Duncan, Juster, and Morgan (1984) show that PSID response rates vary little across a wide variety of socioeconomic and demographic characteristics, and the results of Becketti, Gould, Lillard, and Welch (1988) discussed in Chapter 5, "Data Quality," are also supportive of modest systematic variation in response rates.

Nonsample individuals. The gross flow of individuals into and out of the PSID is far from trivial. As of 1988, more than 37,500 individuals had lived in interviewed *families* at least once since the study began in 1968. About one fifth of this group were born into *sample families* and are considered *sample members* (and given positive weights) by the study staff. Just under one third of the 37,500 had joined panel *families* through marriage, cohabitation, or coresidency either as adults or as the children of such adults. This latter set of individuals is treated as *nonsample* by the PSID and given zero weights, even though they constitute a rich source of potential information. They are not followed once they depart from *sample families*. An alternative procedure would be to develop a weight for them that reflects their chance of falling into the *original sample* and perhaps continue to follow them even if they leave *sample families*. Such weight calculations are not straightforward (see Kalton, 1986; Little, 1989).

The behavioral characteristics of the so-called *nonsample* adults who join *sample families* through marriage or permanent cohabitation were investigated in Becketti et al. (1988) in the context of earnings models. Samples were defined and earnings measured as of the 1981 interviewing year. Separate 1981 earnings functions were estimated for the 2,249 *sample* and 991 *nonsample* male *heads* and for the 1,228 *sample* and 516 *nonsample wives/"wives."* Each group was further broken down into its membership in the *SRC* or *SEO sample*. No significant differences were found between any of the matched *sample-nonsample* pairs. As pointed out in Becketti et al. (1988) and Lillard (1989), this lack of significant difference between *sample* and *nonsample* individuals raises questions about their treatment in weighted analyses. For the time being, their data are assigned a zero weight in any weighted analysis.

Notes

1. For users of the OSIRIS.IV dictionary that accompanies PSID data files, the "not ascertained" code of a full field of 9s is designated as the first

missing-data code (MD1). Most OSIRIS.IV programs automatically exclude values designated as MD1.

2. There are several alternatives to this assumption. For example, retrospective information from a *nonsample* person on his geographic location and family income in 1968 could be used to compute his selection probability from the basic sample design parameters. This technique would be very expensive and would be subject to error due to imperfect recall of conditions in 1968. A working paper by Little (1989), available upon request from the PSID, outlines other possible approaches.

5. Data Quality

For a panel study, issues of nonresponse bias and representativeness of the sample are crucial. Maintenance of high response rates, careful cleaning of the data, and monitoring of data quality are all high priorities for the PSID. Over the years, the board and staff of the PSID have encouraged a number of studies of PSID data quality. The results of these analyses have provided reassuring evidence about the validity of the data and the absence of substantial nonresponse bias.

Response Rates

As noted at the end of Chapter 3, "Field Procedures," the PSID takes a number of special measures to try to ensure high followup response rates. Annual response rates have been exceedingly high in every year except the first. In 1968, the PSID's first year, 76% of sampled families were successfully interviewed. In 1969, interviews were attempted with the heads of family units containing adults who were members of 1968 interviewed families. The response rate in 1969 was 88.5%. Since 1969, annual response rates have ranged between 96.9% and 98.5%. With a minor exception in 1990, no attempt has been made to recontact attriters from previous years. Even small attrition from wave to wave cumulates over time. As of 1988, the response rate for individuals who lived in 1968 households was 56.1%. The level of cumulative response is sufficiently low to raise concerns, and this has prompted direct investigation of possible attrition biases.

Unicon Study

In 1982, the Unicon Research Corporation was commissioned by the National Science Foundation to conduct comparisons of the descriptive characteristics of individuals who had attrited and those still remaining in the panel and to estimate a series of models of earnings, labor supply, and migration using data from early panel waves to see if subsequent attriters differed from respondents in behavioral terms. We quote directly from their results (Becketti et al., 1988, pp. 490-491):

> In this article we examined the dynamics of participation in the PSID and considered whether attrition has affected the representativeness of the PSID. We found some observable variables that are correlated with attrition, but these variables explain only a negligible portion of the attrition in the PSID. We found no compelling evidence that attrition (or entry) has any effect on estimates of the parameters of the earnings equations we studied.
>
> The 1968 PSID is quite unlike the population of the United States if we use the CPS as a benchmark.[1] Weighting the PSID with the weights supplied by ISR goes a long way toward making the PSID sample resemble the CPS sample. While there are statistically significant differences in the empirical distributions of observable characteristics, most of these differences are of no practical significance or can be explained by known differences in coding of answers across the two surveys. For some variables, particularly income and education, there is some reason to believe that the reports in the PSID may be more accurate than those in the CPS. At any rate, the PSID participants behave almost identically, conditional on their observed characteristics, to participants in the CPS.

Lillard-Waite Study of Marital Histories

As part of a larger study of marriage and divorce, Lee Lillard and Linda Waite conducted an analysis of the quality of panel and retrospective marital histories in the PSID. Again, we quote directly from their report (Lillard & Waite, 1989, pp. 252-253):

> Our comparison of panel and retrospective histories produced a detailed picture of the agreements and disagreements between the two. To summarize briefly, we found substantial levels of agreement on marital status as of the first survey interview, and substantial agreement on the occurrence of the first marriage. We found that the dates of first marriage matched best for those who were either married as of the initial interview or who married during the survey in the most typical pattern—living at home until marriage and then moving out. For these people dates from the panel and retrospective histories matched very well indeed.
>
> Disruptions also appeared to be captured well by both types of histories, although we do observe disruptions in the panel that are not reported in the retrospective history and respondents report a substantial number of disruptions that the panel history misses. For those disrupted by both histories, dates of disruption match within a year for three-quarters; we suspect the other quarter are reporting on two different events. . . .
>
> On balance this data set is among the very best for studying the beginnings and ends of marriages. The large sample at all ages, the long panel period, the wealth of other information, and the multiple measures of the events in question all make the PSID an excellent source of information on marriage and divorce.

Curtin, Juster, and Morgan Study of Wealth

As part of a general assessment of the quality of wealth data from surveys presented at the 1988 NBER Conference on the Measurement of Saving, Investment, and Wealth, Curtin, Juster, and Morgan (1988) evaluated wealth data gathered in the 1984 wave of the PSID, the 1983 Survey of Consumer Finances, and the 1984 Wealth Supplement to the Survey of Income and Program Participation (SIPP). A number of quality dimensions were investigated: sample and questionnaire design, response rates and nonresponse bias, ability to represent the upper tail of the income and wealth distribution, the size of measurement error, the importance of item nonresponse and imputations, and the degree to which the household survey adequately represents national wealth. Curtin, Juster, and Morgan (1988) conclude (p. 544):

> 1. Measured against the standards set by previous household wealth surveys, all three of these data sets stand up quite well. They do not differ substantially among themselves when it comes to measuring total wealth and the distribution of wealth in the great bulk of the U.S. population.
>
> 2. The unique design characteristics of the SCF [Survey of Consumer Finances][2] give it the highest overall potential for wealth analysis of the three data sets examined. . . . Comparing PSID to SIPP, one gets a mixed picture, but, in general, PSID had the advantage. Although its basic sample design is less well suited to measuring wealth than SIPP (because it oversamples low-income families, for whom wealth holdings are relatively unimportant), its general descriptive characteristics, taking SCF as the benchmark, look to be closer to actual population characteristics than are those of SIPP. Although PSID is not able to describe the details of wealth holding nearly as well as SIPP because of its highly aggregated nature, its measurement error characteristics look to be consistently better than are those of SIPP. The PSID has a lower item nonresponse rate than SIPP and thus less need to construct imputed values, and it appears to be a somewhat closer match to external control totals.

Other Evidence on Representativeness

Research papers periodically provide additional data on the representativeness of the PSID sample. In an article on PSID data quality, Duncan and Hill (1989) compared 1980 official program totals and PSID reports of aggregate transfer income of various types. They found that the PSID accounted for 92% of income from the Aid to Families with Dependent Children (AFDC) program, 84% of Supplemental Security Income, and 85% of Social Security income. As a frame of comparison, Current Population Survey reports for calendar year 1979 show that the CPS accounts for about 77% of AFDC, 69% of Supplemental Security Income, and 91% of Social Security (U.S. Bureau of the Census, 1983, Table A-2, p. 216). The Census Bureau's Survey of Income and Program Participation does considerably better than the CPS in matching up with program aggregates, accounting for about 79% of Aid to Families with Dependent Children, 94% of Supplemental Security Income, and 101% of Social Security (U.S. Bureau of the Census, 1985, Table D-3, p. 47).

As part of an analysis of the consequences of teenage childbearing, Duncan and Hoffman (1991) compared high school graduation and marriage rates of black and white women in the PSID (at age 25) and the Current Population Survey (at ages 25-29). Although there is some tendency for modest but persistent differences in some of these rates (e.g., black marriage rates are higher in the CPS than the PSID; white schooling rates are somewhat higher in the PSID than the CPS), the trends for both racial groups track fairly closely over the two decades.

As part of a research proposal submitted to the National Institute on Aging, Ken R. Smith compared the mortality experience of the PSID sample from 1968 to 1984 with life tables for the United States taken from 1980 Vital Statistics sources. He found close agreement in the five-year survival rates calculated from the two sources.

Validation Study

A crucial component of the quality of data from any survey such as the PSID is the validity of responses to the questions posed. To investigate this, the National Science Foundation, at the urging of the Board of Overseers, funded a two-wave validation study of the PSID instrument. Attempting to validate responses from actual PSID respondents was judged too costly, so the strategy adopted was to secure the cooperation of a large firm, interview a sample of workers (about 500) from that firm using the PSID instrument, and then, whenever possible, check carefully the responses recorded in the interviews against actual company records.

Evidence from the validation study sample (detailed in Bound, Brown, Duncan, & Rodgers, 1989) shows that the amount of measurement error in cross-sectional reports of annual earnings is rather low, with the ratio of error-to-total variance ranging from .15 to .30, depending on the year of measurement.[3] Error in reports of annual work hours is higher (.28 to .37), while error in reports of hourly earnings, obtained by dividing annual earnings by annual hours, is disturbingly high (.67 to .69).[4]

Although annual earnings were reported fairly reliably, it was also discovered that workers with lower-than-average earnings tended to overreport and high-wage workers to underreport their earnings—a covariance almost always assumed to be zero in measurement error models. This covariance reduced from 18% to 24% the biasing effects due to errors in measuring earnings when earnings is a right-hand independent variable. Mean-reverting error also produced biases to right-hand side variable coefficients when annual earnings is a dependent variable that ranged from 10% to 17%. The restricted variability of true earnings from the single-company sample probably leads to an overstatement of these biases.

Furthermore, the validation data set also showed a surprisingly small decrement to reliability when going from cross-sectional measures of earnings level to panel measures of annual earnings change—there was more "news" than "noise" when earnings were differenced over either one- or four-year intervals.[5] Reliability was also fairly high in panel reports of change in annual work hours. Indeed, apparently turbulent employment conditions produced cross-sectional reports of earnings and hours in one of the survey waves that were *less* reliable than the corresponding change measures.

The company sample also provided validation for retrospective reports over a two-and-a-half-year period of spells of nonemployment with the firm. It showed that *only one third* of the spells of nonemployment appearing in company records were reported in the interviews. Shorter and more distant spells were less likely to be reported, although the fraction of presumably salient longer and more recent spells unreported still exceeded one third. Furthermore, the incidence of reporting error appeared to be correlated with typical right-hand measures such as age and schooling. Thus all of the ingredients for coefficient bias due to measurement errors would appear to be present in unemployment event-history data.

"Seam" Transitions

In 1984, the PSID began coding information on labor force status and program participation on a monthly basis. As has been found in other studies where the measurement period (e.g., month) is less than the length of the reference period (e.g., year), observed transitions tend to concentrate at the beginnings and ends of the reference period. Hill (1987) compared the PSID with the Survey of Income and Program Participation (SIPP) in terms of the disproportionate concentration of transitions at the "seam." Perhaps because of the PSID's longer reference period, he found the extent of seam problems appreciably greater in the PSID than in SIPP data—especially for food stamp recipiency.

Taking advantage of overlap in the 1984 and 1985 PSID reference periods, Hill used dual reports of employment status for the same month to examine individual characteristics associated with "seam amplifying" and "seam attenuating" inconsistencies. Age and race were found to be very strong predictors of seam amplifying inconsistencies—with blacks and older individuals having significantly higher rates of concentration of transitions at seams. Gender and income, on the other hand, were the sole significant predictors of "seam attenuating" inconsistencies—with high-income females exhibiting a greater propensity for this type of response error.

The extent to which these types of response errors affect the estimated parameters of event-history models has not been fully worked out. Hill and Hill (1986), however, have demonstrated that, with SIPP data, whether the week in question is a "seam week" is by far the most important predictor of transitions from unemployment, and the existence of excessive seam (or insufficient within-wave) transitions has profound impacts on the estimated survival functions. It is interesting that, despite a smaller sample size, the chi-square goodness-of-fit statistic of the proportional-hazards model was more than twice as high for the PSID as for the SIPP. This suggests that the original oversampling of low-income and minority households in the PSID has notable analytic advantages.

Taken as a whole, these different studies examine a variety of aspects of data quality, and the general results are supportive of the PSID data being valid and not subject to major nonresponse bias. Still, an analyst of any data set should be sensitive to possibilities of low validity or nonresponse bias for his or her particular analysis.

Notes

1. This refers to the deliberate oversampling of low-income families in the PSID's initial wave.

2. These design characteristics include a long questionnaire focused on components of wealth and an oversample of high-income households.

3. Bound and Krueger (1989) report a similar finding for the March 1977 and 1978 Current Population Survey, using Social Security earnings records for those same individuals for validation.

4. There is no evidence, however, that the measurement errors in measures such as earnings are higher in the PSID than in other surveys. Indeed, the PSID's substantial editing and across-wave consistency checking should make measurement errors of this type less problematic than in surveys not following such procedures.

5. This result held in a CPS-Social Security validation study as well (Bound & Krueger, 1989).

6. Content

Topics

A comprehensive (300-page) listing of the variables available on the PSID's main files is provided as part of the PSID documentation and the *User Guide*; the listing is arranged alphabetically by topic area. Here we can provide only a broad overview of PSID content, some of which has remained constant and some of which has varied during the course of the study. The PSID contains a large number of variables that have been asked about wave after wave in much the same, if not the identical, manner. They constitute what we term *core* PSID content and are available on the main PSID data files. Examples of core content include income, poverty thresholds, family structure, employment, housework, housing, and socioeconomic background. A wide variety of other topics have been covered intermittently in the study. These include, for example, utilities, commuting behavior, child care, wealth, health, and time and money transfers with relatives and friends. Many of the variables based on the intermittent topics are available on the main PSID data files, although some of the fine details have been relegated to special data files.

Both *core* and intermittent variables vary in terms of their time reference: Some refer to the previous calendar year, others refer to the time of interview, and still others refer to some other particular time period specified in the corresponding set of questions. Both *core* and intermittent variables also vary in terms of the reference person, the primary distinctions being *head, wife/"wife,"* other family members, and the family as a whole.

Core content. The *core* content of the PSID is listed in some detail in Table 6.1. Most of this information comes directly from PSID questionnaires and cover sheets. The greatest level of detail on these topics is available for the *head* of the family unit and, in cases where a male head is married to or cohabiting with the same woman for one year or more, the *wife* or long-term cohabitor (termed *"wife"*) of the head.[1] Information about the *wife/"wife"* is more limited in the early years of the study than in the later ones. Throughout the study, a smaller set of information has been collected for family members who were not *head, wife,* or *"wife."*

The timing of many events is recorded as part of the PSID's *core* information. This allows construction of a wide variety of event histories. (See Table 6.2.) Some events can be dated to the month, whereas others can only be dated to the year. The precision of the dating for some events varies through the course of the study, as Table 6.2 indicates. Monthly dating of employment events and income sources began with the 1984 interviewing year, and retrospective marital and childbirth histories collected in the 1985 interviewing year and updated since that time facilitated monthly dating of those events.

Intermittent content. A variety of topics have been addressed by the PSID on a less regular basis than those noted above. These intermittent topics are listed in Table 6.3. During the first five years of the study, an hour-long in-person interview allowed collection of an extensive set of information not well suited to the telephone mode of interviewing in post-1972 waves. Intermittent topics have followed a less regular schedule in the post-1972 period. Since the 1984 wave, the intermittent topics have taken on the qualities of special supplements, each focused on a specific topic and generally included in only one interviewing wave.

34

TABLE 6.1. Core Topics in the PSID[a]

A. Income sources and amounts:
  Earnings of family members
  Business/farm income
  Income from professional practice
    or trade
  Income from farming or gardening
  Income from roomers or boarders
  Income from rent
  Dividends, interest, trust fund,
    royalties
  AFDC/ADC
  SSI
  Other welfare
  Social security
  VA pension, service disability, or
    GI bill
  Retirement pay, pensions, or
    annuities
  Employment compensation
  Alimony
  Child support
  Help from relatives/nonrelatives
  Other income
B. Poverty status:
  Family poverty thresholds[b]
C. Public assistance in the form of
    food or housing:
  Use of food stamps
  Public assistance with housing:
    if in public housing project
    if rent is publicly subsidized
    government assistance with
      heating bills
D. Other financial matters:
  Estimate of federal taxes paid[b]
  Financial assistance to people living
    elsewhere
E. Family structure and demographic
    measures:
  Marital events and status
  Fertility events
  Adopted children
  Number of siblings (total and
    number still living)
  Ethnic group

  Race
F. Employment information:
  Annual and monthly information on
    weeks worked
    weeks unemployed
    weeks out of labor force
    work missed because sick
    work missed because family
      member was sick
    weeks of vacation
    weeks on strike
  For each main job and second job:
    occupation and industry
    whether government worker
    rate of pay on job
    hours per week working
  For each main job:
    whether union worker
    if self-employed, whether
      business is incorporated
  Work experience:
    total
    employer specific
  Employment status:
    employment status at time of
      interview
    whether have been looking for
      work and if so how
  Event-history dating employment
    changes during past year:
    movements between employers
    title changes with the same employer
    occupation and industry
    pay and workload at start and
      end with each employer
    reason for changing employers
G. Housework time
H. Housing:
  Size and type of housing structure
  Whether own home, pay rent, or what
  House value
  Remaining mortgage
I. Geographic mobility:
  Moves during last year—when and
    why

TABLE 6.1. Continued

Plans about moving in future—how certain and why	Race and ethnicity
	Father's occupation
State and county of residence	Parents' poverty status
Where *head* grew up—rural versus urban; state and county	K. Health, religion, military service: General health and disability of
All states head has lived in	family members
Whether head ever moved to take a job	Religious preference
	Ever in military service
J. Socioeconomic background:[c]	L. County-level data:
Education history	Unemployment rates
Parents' completed education	Wage rates for unskilled workers
Number of siblings	Labor market demand conditions

NOTES: a. The amount of detail for these topics is most extensive for the *head* and *wife/"wife"* of the family unit, but some information may be available for other family members as well.
b. Estimates are generated for this information from indirect indicators collected in the annual interviews.
c. Questions regarding an individual's socioeconomic background are asked the first year the individual appears as a *head, wife,* or *"wife"* in an interviewed family unit. this information is *not updated* on a regular basis, although pertinent information may have been gathered subsequently that allows some updating. If the individual switches from a *head* one year to a *wife/"wife"* the next, or vice versa, all of the socioeconomic background questions are reasked. In addition, in a few waves of the study, socioeconomic background information has been asked of all *heads, wives,* and *"wives,"* regardless of whether they are new to that role that year.

Types of Variables

PSID variables vary in terms of source of information and amount of hands-on processing. The variables can be categorized as in Table 6.4, which provides counts of each type of variable.

Family-level variables. Most of the information from any year's data collection is categorized as family-level variables. The family-level variables include not only information that applies to the family unit as a whole (such as total family income or number of children) but also almost all information about the *head* of the family unit and, if present, the *wife / "wife"* as well as a small set of information about the current county of residence. The main PSID files contain about 1,400 family-level variables for the 1988 interviewing year.

About 300 of the 1,400 family-level variables are *edited variables* in the 1988 interviewing year. These variables include income, work hours, remaining mortgage, and family needs. *Edited variables* are considered crucial enough to the overall purposes of the study to

TABLE 6.2. Event Histories Recorded in the PSID

Event	Available Information About the Event
Events with timing recorded to the month:	
Births	Complete birth histories for most PSID individuals, collected 1985 on[a]
Marital status change	Complete marital histories for 1985 *heads, wives,* and *"wives"* plus abridged marital histories for most other PSID individuals, collected 1985 on[a]
Formation and dissolution of cohabitating couples	Gathered for *heads* and *"wives"* as part of every annual interview, 1976 on
Out-of-wedlock births	Can be derived from birth and marital histories for most all PSID individuals, collected 1985 on
Raising of children by nonparents	Complete histories for *heads, wives,* and *"wives,"* collected in 1985[b]
Change in living arrangements, including children leaving home	For all PSID individuals, collected all years of panel for most living arrangements[c]
Change in education	Complete educational histories for *heads, wives,* and *"wives"* (when last attended school; timing of high school diploma, GED, college degree, other degrees or certificates such as vocational or apprenticeship), collected in 1985
Residential moves	For all PSID families, 1975 on (except 1982)[d]
Change in receipt of transfer income	Separately by type of transfer income (including ADC/AFDC, other welfare, *head's* unemployment compensation, *wife's* unemployment compensation, *head's* workers' compensation), 1983 on
Transitions between employment/unemployment/out of labor force	For *head's* unemployment spells, 1981 on; for *wife's* unemployment spells and for labor force transitions for *heads* and *wives,* 1983 on
Change in job/position	For *head* and *wife,* 1983-1987
Change in employer	For *head* and *wife,* 1983 on
Change in second jobs	For *head* and *wife,* 1983 on
Change in occupation	For *head* and *wife,* 1983-1987
Events with timing recorded to the year:	
Change in receipt of public assistance	Based on report of calendar-year assistance given separately by type of assistance

TABLE 6.2. Continued

	(including ADC/AFDC, other welfare, SSI, and food stamps), for all years of panel (except 1983 for food stamps)
Change in poverty	Based on report of calendar-year income and needs, for all years of panel
Transitions between employed/unemployed/ out of labor force	Based on calendar-year reports of work hours and unemployment hours, for all years of panel
Retirement	Based on report of age at retirement, first reported in 1981 for *heads* and in 1983 for *wives/"wives."* Information on annual work hours is gathered every year, providing an alternative way to define retirement
Change in job/position	Captures one change per year, for all years of panel
Change in disability of head	Based on disability status reported at time of interview, for all years of panel except 1973, 1974, and 1976

NOTES: a. In 1985, retrospective histories were collected for 1985 *head, wives, "wives,"* and other family members aged 12-44. In each subsequent year, retrospective histories were gathered for a more limited set of individuals—*heads, wives,* and *"wives"* new to the study in that capacity and family members aged 12-44 who were not *head, wife,* nor *"wife."* Each year beginning in 1986, the histories for prior year *heads, wives,* and *"wives"* have been updated annually for events since the prior year.
b. Dates for the raising of children by a nonparent include only first and most recent spell for any given child/nonparent pair.
c. Relationships between people living together can be more finely distinguished from 1983 on than during 1968-1982.
d. Data capture only one move per year but indicate any changes in county or state.

require special data-quality checks. These variables are reviewed and/or constructed from a detailed set of instructions. About 80 edited variables are considered vital enough to merit special treatment in terms of missing data; imputations are always made for these variables when there is missing data for them. The edited variables with imputations for missing data have an associated variable that indicates the extent of editing done for any given case; this associated variable codes whether major, minor, or no imputations for missing data were made during the processing of the data for that case.

The set of family-level measures, termed *unedited variables* in Table 6.4, is the largest. These variables undergo no special editing.

TABLE 6.3. Schedule of Intermittent Topics in the PSID[a]

1968-1972, 1977-1987: Housing utilities

1969-1986 Commuting to work

1968-1972: Housing and
   neighborhood characteristics
   attitudes and behavior patterns
   do-it-yourself activities
   saving (crude measure)
   disability of family members
   fertility and family planning
   child care
   time use

1972: Achievement motivation
   cognitive ability (sentence
   completion test)

1973-1974: Child care

1975: Neighborhood satisfaction
   and housing problems
   attitudes
   disability of the *head*

1976: Wives' interview
   employment history[b]
   fertility and family planning[c]
   characteristics of job (including
   training required)[b]
   attachment to labor force[b]
   child care[c]
   attitudes[b]

1977: Child care
   disability of the *head*

1978: Job training
   how got jobs
   retirement plans and experiences
   disability of family members

1979: Do-it-yourself activities
   child care
   impact of inflation
   savings (crude measure)
   retirement plans
   disability of the *head*

1980: Time and money help with
   emergencies

food stamp/SSI eligibility
   impact of inflation
   child care
   disability of the *head*
   extended family
   savings (crude measure)

1981-1983: Retirement plans
   (most detail in 1983)
   spells of unemployment/out
   of labor force
   hospitalization over the year
   disability and illness of family
   members

1984: Wealth (level of assets of
   various types)
   fringe benefits
   pension plans and rights
   retirement plans
   inheritances
   savings (crude measure)
   job training
   spells of unemployment/out
   of the labor force
   disability and illness of *head* and
   wife/"wife"

1985: Wives' interview
   retrospective childbirth history[b]
   retrospective history of adoptions[b]
   retrospective history of substitute
   parenting[b]
   retrospective marital history[b]
   retrospective education history[b]
   child care[b]
   housework[b]
   family planning[b]
   disability and illness of *head* and
   wife/"wife"[b]
   job training[b]

1986: General health of all family
   members
   activities of daily living[b]
   hospitalization over the year[b]
   height and weight[b]
   smoking and exercising behavior[b]

TABLE 6.3. Continued

1988: Kinship ties	1989: Wealth (level of assets of various
financial situation of parents	types)
health of parents	saving behavior 1984-1989
time and money help of most kinds	1990: Health and health care of the
	elderly
	links to Medicare records

NOTES: a. The amount of detail for these topics is most extensive for the *head* and *wife/"wife"* of the family unit, but some information may be available for other family members.
b. Questions asked of both *head* and *wife/"wife."*

Examples include home ownership status and current employment status. A small set of family-level variables is calculated by computer from the edited and unedited variables and, in some cases, from previous years' variables. These are known as *generated variables*. These include variables such as income tax, poverty threshold, family weight, number of children of various ages, and identifying information for other families within the same household. A few additional family-level variables take the form of county-level variables. These are based on county-specific information collected from state officials; they apply to the family unit's county of residence at the time of the interview and mostly measure labor market conditions in the area.

Individual-level variables. A small set of individual-level variables is available for each individual who is a member of a family unit

TABLE 6.4. Types of Variables in the PSID

Type of Variable	Number of Variables in 1988 Wave
I. Family-level variables	1,408
A. edited variables	302
B. unedited variables	953
C. generated variables	149
D. county variables	4
II. Individual-level variables	90
A. wave-specific variables	37
B. summary variables	53

interviewed by the study. This set comprises both wave-specific variables and summary variables that may span many years. About 40 wave-specific individual variables are coded each wave for each individual in a family unit interviewed in that wave. These variables cover basic demographic and economic data about an individual. If the individual was *head* of a family unit or the *wife*/"*wife*," much of the information in these variables is also available among the family-level variables, often in substantially greater detail.

Individual-level *summary variables* first appeared with the 1985 wave. Some are based on retrospective historical information. The summary variables include time-invariant information (such as birth weight, identity of parents, and status as a *sample member*), cumulative counts of demographic events (such as number of marriages or number of childbirths), timing of demographic events (such as month and year of various marriages or childbirths), and details about attrition and institutionalization.

Note

1. In the PSID, a cohabitor is labeled a *boyfriend* or *girlfriend* the first wave he or she appears in the study. If that cohabitor is still in that same family unit at the time of the subsequent interview, the cohabitor's label switches to "*wife*" if the cohabitor is female; if the circumstances are otherwise the same and the cohabitor is male, his label switches to *head* and his female partner (who had been *head*) becomes a "*wife*." *Boyfriends* and *girlfriends* are treated like family members who are not *heads* or *wives*/"*wives*," and some information is obtained about them. In waves since the late 1970s, information typically gathered for *wives* has been gathered as well about "*wives*" and that usually obtained for *heads* has been collected for heads living with "*wives*."

7. Data Files

The PSID routinely prepares a number of data files. Most are updated with each new wave of data collection and then made available, along with comprehensive documentation, through the Inter-University Consortium for Political and Social Research (ICPSR).

TABLE 7.1. Types of PSID Data Files

Type of File	Is File Updated with Each Subsequent Wave of Data?	Is File Available Through ICPSR?
Main files:		
Cross-Year Family-Individual Response File	Yes	Yes
Cross-Year Family-Individual Nonresponse File	Yes	Yes
Cross-Year Family File	Yes	Yes
Special public-release files:		
1985 Ego-Alter File[a]	No	Yes
Marital History File[a]	Yes	Yes[b]
Childbirth and Adoption History File[a]	Yes	Yes[b]
Work-History File	Yes	Yes
Relationship file	No	Yes
1988 Time and Money Transfers File	No	Yes
1990 Health Supplement File	No	Yes[b]
Special restricted files:[c]		
PSID-Geocode and Census-Extract Files	No	No
Death Index File	No	No[c]
Medicare Record File	No	No[c]

NOTES: a. The information in these fields can date as far back as the early 1900s, because some histories are for persons who are quite elderly.
b. As of fall 1991, work on this file is still in process but it will be made available to the ICPSR as soon as it is completed.
c. See the final section of this monograph for details about obtaining access to these files.

Most PSID files contain information dating back to the study's first wave and include records for family units, individuals, or pairs of individuals. The types of files are listed in Table 7.1. The files fall into three major categories—main files, special public-release files, and special restricted files.

Main Data Files

Types of main data files. Information gathered in each wave is assembled into data files that contain both current and past information.

- The *cross-year family file* includes only family-level variables and contains *one and only one* data record for each family unit interviewed *in the most recent interviewing wave.*

The information about family units in this file includes family-level information (dating back to 1968) such as total family income and housing tenure as well as details collected about the family unit's *head* and *wife*/ "*wife*" (e.g., occupation and age).

This file has one record for each family interviewed in the most recent wave, multiple records for some families interviewed in previous waves, and no records for some other families interviewed in previous waves. Because new families can be formed when family members move out and set up separate households, a family from a prior wave may be represented by more than one family in the most recent wave. And because entire families attrite, some families from a prior wave will no longer be represented in the most recent wave. The most recent *cross-year family file* contains no information about attriting families. The mixed representation of families from the past is illustrative of problems of using the family (rather than the individual) as the unit of analysis in longitudinal analyses. There are many issues and complexities in defining family units so that the same units can be traced through time. Our general recommendation for longitudinal analyses is to use the individual as the unit of analysis whenever possible; adherence to this recommendation limits the use of the *cross-year family file* in longitudinal analyses.

The size of the *cross-year family file* is a major advantage to analysts with limited computer facilities. The *1968-1988 family file* contains 7,114 records, has an LRECL of 28,744, and occupies 204.4 megabytes. This is about one third the size of the PSID's other cross-year files, making it the file of choice for cross-sectional analysis of the most recent wave with the family as the unit of analysis. In addition, this size difference may be sufficiently advantageous to make an analyst interested in longitudinal analysis want to tackle the challenges presented by the mixed representation of past waves' families.

The PSID has two other types of cross-year files:

- The *cross-year family-individual response file* contains data records for all individuals who are members of PSID family units interviewed in the most recent interviewing wave. Each of these data records includes information (dating back to 1968) both about an individual (e.g., age and sex) and about the families with which he or she has been associated.

Individuals with data records on the cross-year family-individual response file are of three types: (a) those who have been part of a PSID family unit since wave 1 of the study, (b) those born to sample members since the first wave, and (c) those joining a PSID family unit since the first wave in ways other than birth (e.g., marriage). All of these individuals have data values in their *family-level variables* for all years back to and including the first wave.[1] The *individual-level variables* in the records of the born-in or joiners contain a mixture of waves with actual data and waves with no data (waves before they entered the study).

As diagramed in the top panel of Table 7.2, the *cross-year family-individual response file* has one record per individual. It contains information about that individual, gathered each year the individual has participated in the study, as well as information about all of the family units in which the individual has resided over the years.[2] To illustrate the size of this file, the *1968-1988 family-individual response file* contains 20,506 records, has an LRECL of 30,172, and occupies 618.7 megabytes.

A third file, when combined with the *cross-year family-individual* response file, has proven very useful for a variety of longitudinal analyses and for representing the population of families or individuals at some time in the past.

- The *cross-year family-individual nonresponse file* contains information for all individuals who were members of families interviewed in the past but are not members of families interviewed in the most recent wave.

The *cross-year family-individual nonresponse file*, prepared each wave since the 1984 interviewing year and containing variables back through time to 1968, contains the same type of information as the response file but for a different set of individuals—individuals who were part of a family unit interviewed prior to, but not in, the most recent wave.[3] These "nonresponse" persons have left the study for reasons such as death, refusal, or our failure to locate them after a move. The *1968-1988 family-individual nonresponse file* contains 17,022 records, has an LRECL of 30,172 (the same as the 1968-1988 family-individual response file), and occupies 513.5 megabytes.

As shown in Table 7.2, the response and nonresponse versions of the cross-year family-individual file have the same structure (except, of course, the records on the nonresponse file have no data in waves following attrition).[4] The two files can easily be concatenated by the analyst to produce a combined file—

TABLE 7.2. Structure and Content of Records on Cross-Year Family-Individual Files (1968-1988 Cross-Year Family-Individual Response + Nonresponse Files)

	Family-Level Data				Individual-Level Data				Summary Variables
	1968 Data	1969 Data	1970-1987 Data	1988 Data	1968 Data	1969 Data	1970-1987 Data	1988 Data	
Record on Response File (For Individual In a Responding PSID Family 1968-1988)									
	Family Data	Family Data	Family Data	Family Data	Own Data	Own Data	Own Data	Own Data	Data Up to Date as of 1988
Record on Nonresponse File (For Individual In a Responding 1968 PSID Family That Did Not Respond in 1969)									
	Family Data	Filled with Zeroes	Filled with Zeroes	Filled with Zeroes	Own Data	Filled with Zeroes	Filled with Zeroes	Filled with Zeroes	Data Up to Date as of 1968
Record on Nonresponse File (For Individual In a Responding PSID Family 1968-1987 That Did Not Respond in 1988)									
	Family Data	Family Data	Family Data	Filled with Zeroes	Own Data	Own Data	Own Data	Filled with Zeroes	Data Up to Date as of 1987

NOTE: This is a highly simplified depiction of the PSID file structure. Availability of appropriate data for an individual can vary with a number of characteristics of the individual and his or her living arrangements. See the User Guide for details. The size parameters for the 1968-1988 Family-Individual Response File are N=20,506 LRECL=30,172 #Megabytes=618.7. The size parameters for the 1968-1988 Family-Individual Nonresponse File are N=17,022 LRECL=30,172 #Megabytes=513.5.

• *cross-year family-individual response + nonresponse file,* which contains information for all individuals ever part of the PSID study.

This combined file is the file of choice for most purposes, because it enables an analyst to go back to a prior year and gather data about all of the individuals present in that prior year. It is, however, quite large.

Basic structure of main PSID files. Here we provide only general information about how the PSID's cross-year data files are assembled and which ones are best to use for what purpose. We refer the reader to the PSID *User Guide* for a more comprehensive explanation of the file structure.

As explained above, each record in the *cross-year family file* contains family-level data for each interviewing year back to 1968. The yearly interview data in each record are ordered from the earliest interviewing year (1968) to the most recent one. The 1968-1988 file, for example, in effect merges a 1968-1987 family-level history with a 1988 family unit's 1988 data. The 1968-1987 family history is that of the *head* if he is a sample member or that of the *wife/"wife"* if she is a *sample* member and the *head* is not.[5]

For the 1968-1988 file, the family history portion of a record contains a total of 13,117 family-level variables, and the 1988 family-level data consist of 1,408 variables, bringing the total to 14,525 variables in each record on the 1968-1988 family file. The file strings together 14,525 variables for one family, followed by 14,525 variables for another family, on up to the 14,525 variables for the 7,114th family. The variable numbers and tape locations for the family-level variables are listed in the appropriate documentation volumes or machine-readable documentation files and also in the OSIRIS dictionary file.

As shown in Table 7.2, the *cross-year family-individual response file* merges the most recent year of family-level and individual-level variables for an individual with all past years' data for that same person. Each individual's data record is structured so that all of the cross-year family-level variables for that person appear first, followed by all of his or her cross-year individual-level variables.[6]

The *response* and *nonresponse files* are structured identically, and their parallel structures make it easy to concatenate the two files into a single one. We strongly encourage analysts to do this, and, indeed, the frequency distributions printed in our published documentation since the 1984 wave reflect values obtained from the *cross-year family-individual response + nonresponse file*.

The extent to which a particular record on the *cross-year family-individual response* or *nonresponse file* contains actual data in any given wave and the extent to which the data pertain specifically to the given individual and his or her family situation depend on a number of factors. The important factors are

- whether or not, in the given wave, the individual was included in an interviewed family unit (either living in the family or in an institution at the time of interview, or an attriter included in that family in the previous wave);
- if the individual was included in an interviewed family unit, whether he or she (a) was residing in the family unit at the time of interview, (b) was in an institution at the time of interview, or (c) was an attriter since the previous wave;
- if the individual was not included in an interviewed family unit, whether his or her family attrited in the given wave versus in a prior wave;
- whether the individual is an *original sample member*, a born-in *sample member*, or a *nonsample* person who has joined the study since its start; and
- when the person has entered or left the study.

Family-level variables contain data for the interviewed family unit in which an individual is included as of the given wave. If the individual is not included in an interviewed family unit and the given wave is not one that predates his or her entrance to the PSID, then the individual has no family-level data for that wave. (As noted earlier, the family-level history data of the *head* or *wife/"wife"* are merged into individuals' records for waves that predate their initial entrance to the PSID; this filling in with someone else's data is applicable only for *born-in sample members* and *nonsample* persons because *original sample members* have their own family-level histories dating back to the beginning of the study.)

The following individual-level variables contain data, regardless of the individual's PSID status: 1968 FAMILY ID and PERSON NUMBER (identifiers), the wave-by-wave variables TYPE OF INDIVIDUAL RECORD and WHY NONRESPONSE (nonresponse and institutionalization indicators), and many of the individual-level summary variables (including a set that documents key aspects of the individual's history of nonresponse or institutionalization throughout the study). The full set of individual-level variables in a given wave contains actual data if, and only if, the individual was (a) residing in an interviewed family unit at the time of the interview for that wave, (b) was included in an interviewed family but had moved into an institution since the previous wave, or (c) had attrited from an interviewed family since the previous wave. If the individual was included in an interviewed family but had been in an institution since the previous wave, the individual's record contains no individual-level data concerning labor force participation, income, or education for that wave; it does contain data for most other individual-level variables, such as age, gender, and relationship to head. If the individual was not included in an interviewed family in a given wave, his or her record contains no individual-level data specific to that particular wave. The PSID documentation books and *User Guide* provide further details about these aspects of the study.

Special Public-Release Files

Several special public-release files contain detailed information collected by the PSID that would be cumbersome to store on the study's main files. Hence the details have been relegated to special files and the information presented in a more summarized form on the main files. Analysts wanting the complete details on the special topics must turn to these special public-release files. These files may have some stand-alone uses and contain some of the same information as the main files, but they are of greatest value if merged with the main PSID data files. The special public-release files are available through the ICPSR.

Demographic history files. Each year since 1985, the interview has contained questions about a number of demographic events asked of PSID family members eligible for such events. The events include childbirth, adoption, marriage, separation, and divorce. Retrospective histories of substitute-parenting activities were also collected in one wave—1985. Because the full detail on the various demographic events is desired by only a relatively small subset of potential data users, but a sizable number of data users may want some of the detail, we disseminate two types of data products. One is the addition of individual-level summary variables to the main, publicly released PSID data file. These variables include number of marriages, number of childbirths, dates of most marriages, birth dates of most children, identifiers of mother and of father, whether the mother was married at time the individual was born, and birth order of the individual. Creation of several of these variables involves tedious, complex data processing. The other data products are special publicly released, fully documented files containing all present year and past year details of collected demographic history information.

One special public-release file, called the *1985 Ego-Alter file,* contains all of the demographic history detail collected in the 1985 wave. A record on that file represents a pair of individuals related by marriage, childbirth, adoption, or substitute parenting (there is a variable indicating the type of record—marriage record, childbirth record, adoption record, or substitute-parenting record). The demographic history detail from the 1985 wave is based on comprehensive retrospective histories. It includes detail about the timing and circumstances of the demographic event relating the pair of individuals—parenting or marriage—up to and including 1985. The 1985 Ego-Alter file contains 41,368 records, has an LRECL of 82, and occupies 3.3 megabytes.

Other demographic history files are being prepared to provide comparable data that is updated as of the PSID's most recent year of released data. These files cover marital, childbirth, or adoption events separately and build from the 1985 Ego-Alter file, adding events reported since 1985. The files are known as the *Marital History file* and the *Childbirth and Adoption History file.* Like the 1985 Ego-Alter file, these files follow a one-event-per-record format (each record represents a pair of individuals related by the event specified in the file's title—marriage, childbirth, or adoption). Each file is based on retrospective histories dating back to the first event of the specified type and, in many cases, annual updates following the report of a comprehensive history. They differ from the 1985 Ego-Alter file in that (a) there are separate files for the different types of demographic events; (b) individuals reporting zero events of the specified type are included on the file (they were not included on the 1985 Ego-Alter file); and (c) reports of post-1985 events are recorded as are events from retrospective histories reported for individuals entering the PSID since 1985. These separate demographic history files are in preparation and should be publicly available by the time of the printing of this monograph.

Work-History file. This file contains complete information for *heads* and *wives/"wives"* about all of their spells of employment, unemployment, second jobs, and so on reported each wave, beginning with the 1984 wave. Unlike most PSID special files, the Work-History Supplemental file is a stand-alone data file, complete unto itself. With each new wave of data, the Work-History file is rebuilt to include that wave's *entire family record* for all *heads* and *wives/"wives"* along with all of their work history detail. The file also includes a few individual-level variables such as identifiers, SEQUENCE NUMBER, and RELATIONSHIP TO HEAD. Documentation is revised each wave to account for new information. The 1984-1987 Work-History file, to take an example, contains 12,620 records, has an LRECL of 9,566, and occupies 120.7 megabytes.

Relationship file. This public-release file shows the blood, marital, or cohabitational relationship between pairs of individuals up to the 1985 interviewing year. Relationships among all individuals who were members of family units that have descended from a common, original 1968 family unit have been assembled on this file. This file is especially useful for clarifying relationships in the years prior to 1983, when *relationship-to-head* was coded at a one-digit instead of a two-digit level. The Relationship file helps distinguish, for example, stepchildren from biological children. This file can be used to identify relationships of individuals living in separate family units but sharing the same dwelling. It is also useful for identifying an individual's extended kin, whether or not the individual has ever lived with them. Used in combination with the PSID's cross-year files, this file offers the opportunity for rich analysis of living arrangement patterns of "family," broadly defined. The Relationship file contains 426,680 records, has an LRECL of 552, and occupies 235 megabytes.

1988 Time and Money Transfers file. This file contains all of the detail collected in the 1988 wave regarding transfers of time and money help to and from relatives and friends. Each record represents a transfer during the previous calendar year between the interviewed family unit and a relative or friend. The transfer could have been in the form or time or money, and it could have been given to or received from the relative or friend.

1990 Health Supplement. As part of its 1990 interviewing wave, and in conjunction with an NIA-funded project directed by Lee Lillard and Linda Waite of the RAND Corporation, the PSID asked individuals aged 65 or older living in PSID households to sign permission forms for access to Medicare records between 1984 and 1990. When combined with questionnaire information on out-of-pocket medical expenditures and the long time series of core PSID information, the resulting data should be quite valuable for a number of studies on health and well-being of the elderly. The interview portion of these data is being assembled as a special public-release file, called the *1990 Health Supplement file.* A separate file, called the *Medicare Records file,* will contain associated Medicare records, but, because of the confidential nature of the file, it will be released to outside analysts only under special contractual conditions.

Special Restricted Files

The PSID produces several files with access restricted to better assure the confidentiality and anonymity of its respondents. The Medicare Records file noted above is one such file.

PSID-Geocode and Census-Extract files. To test theories that neighborhood of residence exerts a powerful effect on children's success as adults requires data on families at both the neighborhood and the individual levels. To help supply the necessary data, the PSID geocoding project is matching all 33,483 known PSID addresses in the 1968-1985 interviewing years to 1980 and 1970 "neighborhood" areas, allowing analysts to match a wealth of census data on neighborhood characteristics to the family- and individual-level PSID data. This project is funded by the Ford and Rockefeller foundations as well as ASPE/DHHS. Funds for geocoding 1986-1992 PSID addresses have been requested in other proposals.

Tract is identified for addresses in geographic areas that were tracted in the 1980 and 1970 censuses. Containing 4,200 people on average and often formed along "real" neighborhood boundaries, census tracts come closest to approximating the usual conception of a neighborhood. In most states, some nontracted areas (mainly cities in nonmetropolitan areas) were blocked; aggregations of blocks, called Block Numbering Areas (BNAs), provide a reasonable analogue to tracts. In all areas other than tracted and blocked areas, census enumeration district is identified as a "neighborhood" area. Other identifiers include zip code, census place, minor civil division, census county division, metropolitan statistical area, consolidated metropolitan statistical area, FIPS county and state identification numbers, state economic area, and economic subregion.

The PSID-Geocode file contains 34,664 records, has an LRECL of 1,951, and occupies 67.6 megabytes. There are 12 Census-Extract files, each containing data for a different geographic level. The number of records ranges from 22 (occupying 32,428 bytes) to 53,658 (occupying 79,091,892 bytes). Each file has an LRECL of 1,474.

Death Index information. Information from the National Death Index about month and year of death (for deaths occurring after 1993) and cause of death (for deaths after 1983) are expected to be released under contractual conditions as soon as the data can be gathered and documented.

Documentation

Detailed documentation is provided, through the Inter-University Consortium for Political and Social Research (ICPSR), for all PSID data files released to the public. Variables on the main PSID files—the *cross-year family file* and the *cross-year family-individual files* (both *response* and *nonresponse*)—are detailed in the set of documentation books titled *A Panel Study of Income Dynamics: Procedures and Tape Codes*. This multivolume set covers interviewing waves beginning with 1968. The first five waves of data (1968-1972) are documented in the first two books in the set. For each wave starting with 1973, a separate book of documentation has been prepared and made available. Beginning with the 1985 interviewing year, the documentation has been made available in machine-readable as well as printed form.[7]

Each wave's documentation book for the main PSID files contains the questionnaire, a description of the process used for edited variables such as income and work hours, and a complete listing of the code categories for all variables, including missing data codes. Marginal frequencies for the variables are included. Each documentation book also contains an alphabetical index of all variables to date listed by topic area, plus a concordance of all variables available for the given wave of data, listed in the variable number order for that wave. These listings of variables give the variable numbers and tape locations for comparable variables for all waves of the study up to and including the most recent one. They designate the relevant wave and sources of noncomparability, if any, across the waves. Questionnaires are presented in the front of the documentation books. These documentation books are quite comprehensive, and there is no substitute for them for the analyst who wants to discover the details of the data. The most recent documentation book is about 1,000 pages and describes codes and frequency distributions for some 2,000 variables. The 1968-1988 alphabetical index lists more than 15,000 variables.

Separate documentation books are (or soon will be) available for the PSID special public-release files—the 1985 Ego-Alter file, the Marital History file, the Childbirth and Adoption History file, the Work-History file, the Relationship file, the 1988 Time and Money Transfers file, and the 1990 Health Supplement file.

Notes

1. Even though a person was not present in all years of the study, historical information about the PSID family he or she entered has many uses.

2. As in the *cross-year family file*, details for the *head* and *wife/"wife"* are contained in the family unit portion of the data record on the *cross-year family-individual file*. For individuals who are *head, wife,* or *"wife,"* this information duplicates that found in the individual portion of the file.

3. The distinction between the *response* and *nonresponse* version of the *cross-year family-individual files* began with the 1968-1984 cross-year file and has been made for all subsequent *cross-year family-individual files* since then. Prior to the 1984 interviewing year, the *response file* was the only available form of the *cross-year family-individual files*.

4. It is an oversimplification to say that a record on the nonresponse file contains no data in the waves following attrition. It is also an oversimplification to say that a record on the response file contains no data when an individual was an attriter. Because individuals who attrited in the past can reenter interviewed family units, records on both the response and the nonresponse files can intersperse waves with actual data and waves with no data.

5. An exception to this rule concerns the situation of a son or daughter, call him or her X, who leaves the parental family, sets up a separate household, attrites, and then moves back to the parental family. Individual X and his or her spouse will receive X's family history rather than that of the *head* or *wife/"wife."*

6. Although family-level variable numbers and tape locations remain invariant across waves, individual-level variable numbers and tape locations change from wave to wave. To obtain the correct individual-level variable numbers, always consult the documentation volume corresponding to the most recent year of data on your data file.

7. The ICPSR routinely distributes the printed form of documentation. Machine-readable documentation for recent waves is available from them upon request.

8. Data Analysis

PSID data have proven useful for an incredibly diverse set of cross-sectional and longitudinal analyses. Before presenting examples of analyses based on the PSID data, we first discuss several key elements relevant to analysis and provide information about what types of analysis the various data files are best suited to perform.

Key Analysis Issues

The following questions are important to address before doing an analysis of the PSID:

- What is the appropriate unit of analysis?
- How can family composition change influence the variables and/or the sample?
- What variables are available and how are they constructed?
- Should the data be weighted?
- What data-quality issues should be taken into account?

- Are the estimates of sampling errors and standard errors provided in most statistical programs appropriate?
- Should all cases be used from the start, or should some of them be saved for a final test of the model?

Each of these issues is explored below.

Unit of analysis. The PSID allows wide variety in the choice of unit of analysis. It can be used to represent individuals, couples, families, person-years, couple-years, or ex-couple years. It can represent the U.S. population as a whole or subgroups of the U.S. population, including race, sex, and age subgroups as well as residents of major regions of the country (e.g., South or West). Due to its clustered sample design, it cannot, however, properly represent individual states, cities, or similar small geographic divisions.

Although the term "individual" needs little clarification, the term "family" is more ambiguous. The PSID's initial definition of a family was similar to that used by the Census Bureau—a group of individuals living together who are related by blood, marriage, or adoption. Like the Census Bureau, the PSID has never treated lodgers, conventional roommates, or employees who share the housing unit as members of its families. Unlike the Census Bureau, the PSID has never distinguished "unrelated individuals" from families; they are treated as single-person families. Over time, the Census Bureau and PSID definitions of families have diverged in one important respect: the treatment of "cohabitors." The PSID has come to include unmarried couples as part of the same family if the couple is living together in what appears to be a fairly permanent arrangement. If the cohabitation extends for more than one interview, the PSID treats cohabitors as though they were spouses by asking them the same question sequences as married couples. For the Census Bureau, an unmarried cohabitor is part of the "household" but not part of the "family."

Although, at any particular time, it is relatively straightforward to assemble individuals into families, defining longitudinal families—the same family over time—is much more difficult. If the wife leaves, taking some of the children, which of the two new units is the same family? The individual is a unit better suited to longitudinal analysis than the family, but it is often important to consider the individual in the context of the family he or she is part of at different times (Duncan & Hill, 1985).

Family composition change. Most analyses of PSID data must consider possible implications of family composition change. Even cross-sectional analyses can be affected, because not all family measures taken at the time of the interview hold for that point in time or, indeed, for the same interval of time. Annual family income and annual family needs, for example, are flows over time, and both refer to the calendar year *preceding* the time of the interview, not the year of interview. Changes in family composition between the prior calendar year and the time of the interview are certainly possible, and hence the family members present at the time of interview may be more, fewer, or the same number as during the prior calendar year. Measures such as family size and marital status of the head are point-in-time measures taken at the time of the interview.

Family composition change can play an especially important role in longitudinal analyses. A vital point to keep in mind regarding the PSID is that it tracks both individuals and families. This is often a distinct advantage, but the importance of maintaining clear distinctions between family units and the individuals within them when analyzing PSID data cannot be overemphasized.

There is a surprising amount of family composition change from one year to the next. Little was known about this when the study started, and, as the study has progressed, the cumulative level of family composition change has become quite striking. Nearly one quarter of the PSID's families experience at least some type of change in a typical year, and only about 1 in 20 remained completely unchanged for the first 18 years of the study. Couples divorce, spouses die, children grow up and leave home, and new children enter families at birth or adoption. These life-cycle changes are routine. More complicated changes include children leaving home in "false starts" (later returning to their parental home); married couples separating for a few years and then reuniting (or divorcing and remarrying each other later); grandchildren, aunts, nephews, or other relatives moving into or out of the family; and children being born to one of several unmarried daughters or sons still living in his or her parental home. These changes can have profound implications for analysis of the PSID, especially if the analysis involves two or more waves of data. Some of these implications are simply annoying complications to the structure of the data, but many of them raise substantive issues that analysts must address. Examples follow.

- A number of variables available in any wave t of the data have been developed to account for family composition change occurring between waves t − 1 and t. Such measures include annual family income of all types and annual family needs. It is important for the analyst to understand how they are constructed to best match them with measures of family structure.

- The very concept of the family loses its traditional meaning when placed in a dynamic context. For example, if there is a divorce, then a single family becomes two families—a "family" of the ex-husband and a "family" of the ex-wife. If one wants to describe changes in the economic status of families, then which family is to be thought of as the "same" family?

- Relationships defined by family status (e.g., *wife, child*, or *head*) are unique at one time but not across time.

- Longitudinal analyses over several years are most naturally conducted on individuals who were living in responding families during all of those years. But one might want to include individuals who died or attrited, or children who were born during the period under investigation.

Even if these substantive issues are not relevant, technical problems caused by family composition changes can be substantial. Examples follow.

- The *head* (or the *wife* / *"wife"*) of a family may not be the same in wave t as in wave t + 1 or wave t − 1. One should not try to relate the hourly earnings reported by a young male *head* in 1987 to the educational attainment of the male *head* in 1976. The young man's father may have been the head of the 1976 family in which the young man was residing. *Although changes in the family head can be recognized readily in the PSID data, they have caused serious errors in analysis.* It is important that analysts understand the implications of these changes for the structure and interpretation of the data.

- Not all individuals living in a family in year t share the same family history. If a couple has reunited after a separation of several years, the family-level variables (such as annual family income) for those years of separation will differ for the two individuals.

- In the PSID, there may be multiple family units within the same household, and this may be important to take into account. PSID variables record the existence of such situations. In some cases, the designation of separate family units within the same household is merely an artifact of the PSID's tracking rules. Some individuals who set up independent households during the panel period subsequently return to their original households (as when a child leaves the parental home for a new home of his or her own and then returns to the parental home). Split-offs such as these (with one type of exception) continue to be interviewed as separate family units, even after they return to their original households.[1] The PSID includes variables on the data files that indicate multiple-family units sharing the same dwelling unit and the identity of the family units involved.

Construction of variables. The PSID documentation should be studied closely when choosing and recoding PSID variables. Aspects of variables that are especially important to keep in mind are as follows:

- *Reference period*: Some of the information gathered in the year t interview refers to calendar year t – 1, but other information refers to the situation of the family at the time of the year t interview. For example, the head's occupation at the time of interview may be "accountant" but his annual labor earnings for the previous calendar year are from a period during which he was a full-time student. It may be necessary to realign information from two different interviewing waves. A check of question wordings or headings for variables in the yearly documentation's tape codes provides information on whether the present or the past is the frame of reference.

- *Across-time completeness and consistency*: If data from several interviewing waves are used, it is important to check the variables for any inconsistencies in code categories or for gaps in availability of the measures in the full span of waves.

- *Background measures*: Values for variables from the *Background Section* of the questionnaire (asked of *new head* or *new wife/"wife"*—a person in the designated family position in wave t who was not in that family position in wave t − 1) are not updated annually; hence these variables need to be treated carefully. Questions in the *Background Section* on retrospective work history, asked of *heads* after 1985, for example, have been asked only of *new heads* each year. Beginning in 1983, a family-level variable has been coded each year indicating when the *head* of the family most recently became a *new head* and thus answered the background questions.

- *Measures requiring special understanding*: Measures of such things as poverty, disability, religious preference, taxes, education, transportation, and geographic characteristics often have precise definitions that may or may not correspond closely with constructs available from the PSID. The *User Guide* offers guidance about handling the pitfalls in defining such variables.

- *City size and urban/rural measures*: Differences between the PSID and other studies, including those by the Bureau of the Census, in geographic delineators and variable definition can mean noncomparability in city size or urban/rural measures.

Data quality issues. There are also aspects of data quality that may be important to analysis design.

- *Proxy respondents*: Only one person per family unit provides an interview in a given year, and that person is generally, but not always, the *head* of the family unit. If any key variables in an analysis (e.g., attitudes) require that the *head* be the respondent, then the analyst needs to subset the data to eliminate cases with someone other than the *head* as the respondent. Missing-data codes do not necessarily indicate that a variable labeled as a *head* variable or one labeled as a *wife/"wife"* variable contains information supplied by that specific person. The identity of the respondent is indicated by a family-level variable called WHO WAS RESPONDENT (V16128 in 1988).

- *Seemingly valid data for persons not in interviewed family units*: What appears to be valid data may be present on the family-level and individual-level portions of an individual's data record for a given wave even if that individual was not residing with an interviewed PSID family at the time of interview.

A family member who at the time of interview is in an institution (e.g., college, the armed forces, jail) or who moved out of the family, or died, since the previous interview will have both family-level and individual-level data on his or her record for that wave. If such a *mover-out* does not return to a PSID family by the next wave of interviewing, the person is then classified as a *nonresponse* individual and (with a few exceptions)[2] both the family-level and the individual-level variables have no data for that and all subsequent waves unless and until he or she returns to a PSID family. If a PSID family cannot be interviewed in a wave, all members are classified as *nonresponse* individuals in that wave and (with the same few exceptions) their records have no family-level and individual-level data for that wave.

A person who entered the PSID after 1968 (but not as part of the *Latino subsample*)[3] has both family-level and individual-level data for the wave of entry, but his or her record also carries family-level data back to the beginning of the study. This historical *family-level* data is identical to that of the *head* of the family unit that he or she first enters (with the exceptions noted in the "Basic Structure of Main PSID Files" section in Chapter 7). The *mover-in's individual-level* variables prior to the wave of first appearance contain no data (with a few exceptions).[4] Storage of the historical family-level data in the *mover-in's* record facilitates some types of analysis, such as describing the poverty history of a child's mother prior to the child's birth and relating that poverty history to the child's birth weight.

The method of distinguishing among these various instances of persons not present in the family at the time of interview is detailed in this chapter's "Key Variables" section.

- *Missing data*: The PSID's treatment of missing data varies across its variables. Most of the income and work hours variables have been "edited" by the study staff, with values imputed when data were missing. These variables have accompanying ACCURACY CODE variables that record, on a case-by-case basis, the extent of editing. For most other measures, no assignments have been made for missing data but there are distinct code categories in the variable that indicate missing data.

- *Extreme values*: Very large or small values can be reported on PSID variables such as income. It can be unclear whether these reflect true values, and, even if they do, the values can be so extreme or the person to whom they pertain can have such a large weight in an analysis that those values can dominate results. In some situations, field-width constraints have produced a few truncated values. Extreme values on variables create a problem that is not unique to the PSID but that is something to be considered in analysis of any data set. The analyst may want to truncate extreme values or omit the cases with the extreme values.

Weighting the data. Decisions about weighting the data can be difficult. There are four reasons that unweighted estimates made from PSID data might not correspond to U.S. population totals.[5] (Each of these was discussed at greater length in earlier chapters.) First, the initial sample consisted of about 3,000 families chosen from a Survey Research Center self-weighting probability sample and about 2,000 low-income families that had previously been interviewed as a part of another study. Second, the dynamics of family composition change produce a larger proportion of young family units and individuals than appears in the population as a whole. Thus even the SRC cross-section portion of the sample has become "overloaded" with the young and will not produce unbiased estimates of simple population parameters unless weighted. Third, there has been some differential attrition over the years. Fourth, immigrants have joined the population of the United States since 1968, and, although a *Latino subsample* was added to the PSID in 1990, other groups of immigrants are not well represented.

Although the PSID cannot be adjusted in a way that makes its sample entirely representative with respect to recent immigration, it can be adjusted in ways that help overcome the other three problems. Weight variables (one at the family level and one at the individual level) have been constructed each year to account for the effects of initial oversampling of some subgroups, expansion over time in the proportion of younger families in the study, and differential attrition.

When should the data be weighted? Clearly, weights should be used whenever the analyst uses cases from both the SRC and the SEO subsamples to estimate simple population parameters such as means, variances, or simple correlations between variables. If such estimates are not based on the weights, then they describe only what is true for the PSID sample and not what is true for either the population as a whole or for any subgroup within the population. If the analyst wishes to use the data to estimate a properly specified multivariate model, the case for weighting is less compelling, because the model presumably controls for the effects of the factors that lead to the need for the weights in the first place. (An exception to this is when the dependent variable of the model is income, earnings, or some other measure directly related to the PSID's oversampling criteria. In this case, there is no justification for including the low-income subsample if weights are not used.)

A researcher can always analyze the *cross-year family-individual response file* using the most recent individual weights in combination with the appropriate filters on the RELATIONSHIP TO HEAD variables and obtain unbiased estimates of finite population parameters. Analyses of individuals are, in general, most easily performed using the *cross-year family-individual files* and weights. Analyses using individuals from the *cross-year family-individual response + nonresponse files* are not as tricky as might be feared. Each individual has an assigned individual weight for each wave in which he or she is present in the sample. If an individual attrites at some point, however, a zero individual weight is assigned to the waves after the point of attrition. Fortunately, the individual weights are scaled for each wave so that they are compatible across waves.[6] Thus one can use the individual weight associated with the most recent wave in which an individual contributes data to a particular analysis, even if the "most recent wave" differs across individuals in the analysis.

In summary, unbiased estimates can always be obtained using the combined SEO and SRC portions of the PSID sample along with the most recent individual weights and the appropriate filters on RELATIONSHIP TO HEAD. It is possible to obtain unbiased estimates of multivariate statistics without weighting by using only the SRC cross-section portion, but the analyst would have to account explicitly for all the selection processes (differential sampling fractions, attrition, death, and family composition change). Finally, it is never appropriate to use the weight variables that appear on the PSID files in independent analyses of either the SRC or the SEO subsamples. Rules for sample selection and weighting are summarized in Table 8.1.

Sampling errors and design effects. In analysis of survey data, it is generally desirable to assess the reliability of the estimates in terms of sampling variation, or "sampling errors." Although many standard statistical computer programs provide measures of sampling errors, they assume the use of a simple random sample (SRS) and can be deceptive when the sample does not satisfy that criterion.

The PSID sample (and the samples of virtually all other national studies of this kind) departs from a simple random sample by being a stratified multistage sample. It consists of two samples that could overlap, and both of the underlying samples involved stratification (selections from partitions, or strata, of the population) and clustering (where primary sampling unit areas are selected, then areas within each of them are defined and selected, and so on, ending with several addresses along selected blocks). These departures from simple random sampling have different effects on the degree to which sampling errors obtained from standard software diverge from sampling errors that take account of the design. Stratification reduces the sampling variance relative to simple random sampling, whereas clustering increases it. (See Kalton, 1979; Kish, 1965; Lansing & Morgan, 1971, pp. 71-75; Wolter, 1985.) The reduction in sampling variance by stratification is greatest when the strata are most dissimilar; the increase from clustering is least when the individuals within the cluster are most dissimilar. The degree of similarity or homogeneity within clusters varies, depending on what characteristic is being examined. Within-cluster homogeneity is high for characteristics such as race of respondent because of the high degree of racial segregation in the United States. On the other hand, there may be little or no geographic clustering on characteristics such as height or birth date of respondent.

Calculating sampling errors in ways that take account of the stratified multistage features of the PSID design is more cumbersome and expensive than the simple random sampling approaches of standard software. General-purpose tables illustrating the range of sampling errors and design effects (the ratio of the actual variance of the estimate to the variance computed for a simple random sample of the same size) by type of statistic—mean, proportion,

TABLE 8.1. Appropriate Sample Selection and Weighting Strategies for Various Types of Multivariate Analyses[a]

Type and Unit of Analysis	Most Recent Family File and Most Recent Family Weight	Most Recent Family-Individual Response File and Most Recent Family or Individual Weight[b]	Most Recent Response + Nonresponse Family-Individual Files and Individual Weight Associated with Most Recent Year of Data Used
Cross-sectional estimates for families in most recent year	Including all families in the most recent year and weighting gives unbiased estimation with the largest possible number of cases.[cd]	Restricting sample to individuals who *head* families in the most recent year and using most recent family weight gives unbiased estimates with largest possible number of cases.[cde]	There is nothing gained by using the nonresponse file for this purpose.
Cross-sectional estimates for *heads* or for *wives/"wives"* in most recent year	Including families in the most recent year and weighting gives unbiased estimation with the largest possible number of cases.[cd]	Restricting sample to individuals who are *heads* or are *wives/"wives"* in most recent year and using most recent family weight gives estimates based on the largest possible number of cases. Restricting sample to *heads* or *wives/"wives"* who are *sample* and weighting by the individual weight yields unbiased estimates based on fewer cases but avoids the assumption that individuals marry persons with identical selection probabilities.[cde]	There is nothing gained by using the nonresponse file for this purpose.
Change estimates for family-level measures from a prior year to most recent year[f]	Usually appropriate if sample is restricted to families with no changes in *head* or *wife/"wife"* —e.g., there is no radical change in the unit of measurement.[cd]	Usually appropriate if sample is restricted to individuals living in families with no changes in *head* or *wife/"wife."* To represent families, restrict sample to *heads* and use family weight. To represent individuals, use individual weight.[cde]	There is nothing gained by using the nonresponse file for this purpose.

TABLE 8.1. Continued

Type and Unit of Analysis	Most Recent Family File and Most Recent Family Weight	Most Recent Family-Individual Response File and Most Recent Family or Individual Weight[b]	Most Recent Response + Nonresponse Family-Individual Files and Individual Weight Associated with Most Recent Year of Data Used
Cross sectional estimates for families in a prior year	Inappropriate	Inappropriate	Restricting sample to *heads* in the prior year and using the family weight for that prior year gives unbiased estimates.[cd]
Cross-sectional estimate for individuals in a prior year	Inappropriate	Inappropriate	Restricting sample to individuals present in the prior year and using the individual weight for that prior year gives unbiased estimates.[cde]
Longitudinal estimates for individuals	Inappropriate	Appropriate if the analyst is interested in a time frame that requires individuals to be present in the most recent wave. Weighting with the individual weight and using the individual as unit of analysis gives unbiased estimation.[cde]	Restricting sample to individuals present in the appropriate years and using the individual weight from the most recent year that a given individual

64

Intergenerational analysis	Inappropriate	Restricting sample to individuals who were children initially and using most recent individual weight gives unbiased estimation but smaller sample sizes than would be possible with the response + nonresponse file.[cd]	...contributes data gives unbiased estimation.[cde] Restricting sample to individuals who were children initially and using the individual weight from the most recent year that a given individual contributes data gives unbiased estimation with maximum sample size.[cd]

NOTES: a. Weighting is always recommended for univariate and bivariate description. In this table, "most recent" refers to the most recent year on the data file available to the analyst.

b. The individual weight is zero for *nonsample* individuals.

c. Weighting can be ignored if the analyst models inclusion probabilities and restricts the sample in the manner specified. The probability of inclusion is a function of the initial selection probability and differential attrition. Initial selection probabilities for the SRC subsample cases are identical.

d. If the dependent variable is related to income and weights are not used, then the SEO subsample of families or individuals should be filtered out.

e. Analysts who wish to include *nonsample* individuals (who have an individual weight of zero) to maximize the number of observations may want to test for differences in parameter estimates between *sample* and *nonsample* individuals.

f. We recommend that the analyst consider reformulating analysis to use the individual rather than the family as the unit of analysis.

regression coefficient—can be helpful in assessing the extent to which actual sampling errors are likely to differ from sampling errors computed under simple random sampling assumptions. There are several ways to estimate proper sampling errors. For example, "collapsed stratum" methods can be used for estimating sampling errors for means and proportions as well as multiple classification analysis (MCA) statistics. More complex methods involving repeated replication procedures can be used to calculate sampling errors for regression statistics. (See Kalton, 1979, for a more complete discussion of these techniques.)

All such variance estimation techniques rely on classifying the geographically defined primary sampling units (PSUs), created when the sample was first selected, into a set of mutually exclusive and exhaustive units known as sampling error computing units (SECUs). These SECUs are then classified into mutually exclusive and exhaustive subsets known as strata. Beginning with the 1983 interviewing year, the PSID's *cross-year family-individual files* have included variables representing SECU and stratum for each case.

The PSID data file contains two variables, the PSALMS STRATUM and PSALMS SECU, which code the stratum and SECU to be used in paired-, multiple-, or successive-differences computations. The stratum variable has values ranging from 1 to 54. Strata 1 to 53 contain paired SECUs; there are exactly two SECUs in each, coded 1 or 2 in the PSALMS SECU variable. Stratum 54 contains 115 SECUs and corresponds to the multiple- or successive-differences computational approach. The "PSALMS" designation in the variable name refers to a sampling error program in the OSIRIS.IV system that uses paired-, multiple-, and successive-differences computations to estimate sampling variances for means, proportions, and totals. There are several other mainframe software packages available that compute sampling errors for stratified multistage samples: SESUDAAN (Shah, 1981) and SUPERCARP (Hidiroglou, Fuller, & Hickman, 1980). There are also microcomputer-based packages available, SUDAAN (Shah, La Vange, Barnwell, Killinger, & Wheeless, 1989) and PC CARP (Fuller, 1986), for example.

There is an alternative approach to estimating sampling variances based on pseudo- or repeated replications (see Kish & Frankel, 1970; or McCarthy, 1966, for a more complete discussion).

In these approaches, repeated overlapping subsamples of SECUs, or replicates, are selected from the sample SECUs. For each replicate, and for the total sample, an estimate of the statistic of interest (e.g., a regression coefficient) is computed. The sampling variance of the estimate for the total sample is computed as the variability of replicate estimates around the total sample estimate.

A specific set of replicates, called "balanced repeated replicates," or "balanced half-samples," reduce the number of subsamples needed in computation. In the balanced set of half-samples, each stratum contains exactly two SECUs, and half-sample replications are created by selecting one of the two SECUs from each stratum. Balancing reduces the number of replications needed for calculating the sampling errors and is accomplished by selecting certain of the half-samples for the replicates.

Balanced half-samples variance computation requires that there be exactly two SECUs per stratum. The PSID data contain another set of variables for which such pairing has been done, the balanced repeated replication (BRR) stratum and BRR SECU variables. The PSALMS strata and SECUs have been regrouped to make the pairs necessary for the BRR technique.

This discussion gives only a brief overview of the features of sampling variance estimation for stratified multistage samples. The interested reader is encouraged to examine the references given earlier for more details.

Hill (1981) illustrates typical sampling errors for an analysis commonly done with PSID data—earnings regressions estimated separately for the four primary race/sex subgroups. Design effects associated with PSID data generally lead to a net increase in the actual sampling error relative to simple random sampling. Hill's results show ratios of actual standard error to standard error assuming simple random sampling that range from 0.95 to 2.53, with most in the range 1.1 to 2.2 and only one less than 1.0. The increase in sampling error is especially pronounced among clustered subsamples such as blacks, the poor, or black women workers. Analyses that include multiple members of the same families can also involve large design effects, particularly if either the outcome or the predictors are family-level measures applicable to a time when the individuals resided in the same families. Such situations add yet another level of clustering, the clusters being the families. Analyses involving clustering within families, such as analyses of parental effects on the attainments of children, can have much larger design effects than those reported here.

Split-sample hypothesis testing. Standard statistical tests are not valid if the analyst has "searched" through the data before arriving at the final specification of the model. For each wave, there is a SPLIT-SAMPLE FILTER variable (a family-level variable) that can be used to divide the sample into independent quarters.[7] The analyst can then use one quarter, one half, or three quarters of the data to develop a suitable model and then test the final model on the remaining portion of the sample.

Key Variables

Several sets of individual-level variables are important in most analyses of the PSID's family-individual data files. One set of variables is fixed over time and constitutes the unique identifier for an individual; this is important for linkages between any special files and the main files and for matching records of relatives. The other variables are wave specific and are key to identifying the appropriate sample to use.

Two variables, used in combination, constitute the unique identifiers for individuals in the study: 1968 FAMILY ID (the identification number for the family unit the individual was part of in 1968 or has since become associated with) and PERSON NUMBER (a 1968 individual-level variable that uniquely identifies the various people associated with a given 1968 family unit). Ranges of values on PERSON NUMBER also convey information of use to the analyst. These ranges[8] are as follows:

001-019	Individuals who were living in *sample families* at the time of the wave 1 interview
020	Husband of the wave 1 *head* who was living in an institution at the time of the wave 1 interview
021-026	Wave 1 *children of head* who were under 25 and living in institutions at the time of the wave 1 interview
030-169	Individuals entering PSID family units as newborns after the wave 1 interview and who had at least one *sample* parent in the study at the time of their birth; these persons are *sample members*

170-226   Individuals who first moved into the study after the wave 1 in-
           terview or entered PSID family units as newborns after the
           wave 1 interview but had no *sample* parent in the study at the
           time of their birth; these persons are not *sample members*
227-228   Husband or wife of wave 1 *head* who moved out or died in the
           year prior to the wave 1 interview
400-499   A variety of *nonsample* individuals aged 65 or older who are
           treated as if they were *sample members* starting as early as the
           1990 wave[9]

A variable that might easily win the title of "Most Useful PSID Variable" has the rather nondescript label of SEQUENCE NUM-BER. It appears in each wave's set of individual-level variables, and nonzero values are assigned to it in a given wave if the given individual is a member of a responding family or has ei-ther died or moved out of the PSID but with a responding family to report the event. As each wave's completed questionnaires ar-rive to be coded, one of the first processing tasks is to assign a SEQUENCE NUMBER to each individual who moved into, out of, or continued to reside in a family interviewed that wave. The "sequence" part of this variable's label refers to the order of a given family unit's members, ranking them on the basis of their RELATIONSHIP TO HEAD in that family unit in that wave. Ranges of code values for SEQUENCE NUMBER are meaningful, as are the distinct values for the variable. The ranges are as fol-lows, where t designates the given interviewing wave:

01-20   Individual present in a wave t responding family unit
51-59   Individual in an institution (i.e., college, the military, jail, or a
         hospital) at the time a wave t interview is taken with his or her
         family unit
71-80   Individual who, between wave t − 1 and wave t interviews,
         moved out of a wave t responding family unit or out of an institu-
         tion but is not a member of any wave t responding family unit
81-89   Individual who was living in a family unit interviewed in wave t
         but who died between the wave t − 1 and the wave t interviews
00   Individual who is not a member of any wave t responding fam-
         ily unit and was either lost to the study by the wave t − 1 inter-
         view or whose family unit became lost to the study between
         wave t − 1 and wave t, or who had not yet appeared in a PSID
         family unit by wave t

To restrict an analysis of the *cross-year family-individual files* to individuals who were actually present in the family at the time of the interview, include only those individuals with SEQUENCE NUMBER in the 1-20 range for that wave. To restrict an analysis of the *cross-year family-individual response file* to *current wave families*, include only individuals who, in the most recent wave, had a SEQUENCE NUMBER equal to 1 (*head*).

Another very useful variable is RELATIONSHIP TO HEAD, an individual-level variable that describes the individual's relationship to the *head* of his or her family unit in a given wave. In waves 1968 through 1982, this variable was coded at a highly aggregated level, with a total of 9 code values. Since 1983, the code values for RELATIONSHIP TO HEAD have spanned 34 categories. Most analysts will never need to use the details built into this variable and will be content with the major categories of *head, wife* (presumed to be the legal spouse of the head), *"wife"* (spouselike female partner who has been cohabiting for more than one wave), children, and perhaps grandchildren. But the detail is there for analysts desiring it.

A set of individual-level variables providing details about nonresponse or being in institutions are these: TYPE OF INDIVIDUAL RECORD and WHY NONRESPONSE. The TYPE OF INDIVIDUAL RECORD variable helps convey the extent to which valid-data versus zeroed-data values are to be expected in a record for that wave's variables. It combines information about the individual being

(1) *sample* versus *nonsample*,
(2) in a responding family versus a member of a responding family but in an institution versus being one of several types of attriters, and
(3) eligible for tracking when moving to a new family unit.

The WHY NONRESPONSE variable helps identify all known deaths, other specific reasons for attrition (such as refusal or inability to locate) as well as type of institution an individual is in (e.g., college, jail, hospital, military) or not yet entering the study.

Which Files for What Analysis?

Analysis possibilities for the PSID include cross-sectional analyses based on a single wave of data, cross-sectional analyses based on multiple waves of data, and a variety of longitudinal approaches. Examples of these various approaches include

- describing or modeling individual change in measures of interest;
- averaging a measure over several years to reduce the effects of random errors of measurement or of transitory fluctuations;
- taking different measures from different years (because not all questions were asked in every year);
- using the long series of year-to-year reports of rare events to construct "event histories" of various demographic and economic behaviors;
- relating, for large numbers of individuals who were children in the first year of the study, their own reports of attainments in adulthood to the characteristics of the family in which they grew up, reported by their parents during those years;
- pooling several years of data to perform "pooled cross-section time-series" analyses;
- pooling pairs or triplets of years, perhaps surrounding an event of interest (such as divorce, death, or childbirth) to look at antecedents or consequences of the event;
- matching ex-husbands and ex-wives to examine the comparative effects of divorce and the potential for larger child support transfers; and
- matching siblings to estimate "sibling" models that are designed to determine the effects of parental background on attainment.

The PSID's design is complex because of its multipurpose nature and because there is enormous diversity in the experiences of PSID members (if it can happen, it will in our study!). This means that adapting the data files to particular purposes can be quite complicated. Data analysis is easiest when using only the most recent wave's information and treating it as a single year of cross-sectional data. But analysis possibilities are greatly expanded by the availability of multiple waves of data at both the family and the individual levels.

Table 8.2 outlines the major types of analyses possible with PSID data files and notes which of the main PSID data files is most suitable for which types of analysis. Although the *cross-year family-individual response + nonresponse files* can be used for *all* analyses, the resulting file is extremely large and, as Table 8.2 shows, in many cases, a smaller file can be used. Sometimes the smaller file is the one best suited to the analysis, and sometimes special care must be taken with the smaller file to ensure that it

72

TABLE 8.2. Types of Analyses and Appropriate PSID Data Files

| Unit of Analysis | Appropriate Main PSID Data File | | |
	Cross-Year Family	Cross-Year Family-Individual Response	Cross-Year Family-Individual Response + Nonresponse
Cross-sectional analysis, using single wave:			
Families in most recent year	Recommended	Recommended	Possible but inefficient
Individuals in most recent year	For *heads* and *wives/"wives"* only	Recommended	Possible but inefficient
Families in past year	a	a	Recommended
Individuals in past year	a	a	Recommended
Cross-sectional analysis, using multiple waves:			
Families	b	a	Recommended
Individuals	b	a	Recommended
Longitudinal:			
Individuals responding in all years being analyzed, including most recent year	b	Recommended	Possible but inefficient
Individuals responding in all years being analyzed, not necessarily most recent year	b	b	Recommended
Individuals who were either *head* or *wife/"wife"* in most recent year and some past year(s)	b	Recommended	Possible but inefficient
Histories of individuals responding in most recent year	b	Recommended	Possible but inefficient
Person-years at risk, not necessarily most recent year[c]	b	a	Recommended
Parent and adult-child pairs	b	a	Recommended

NOTES: a. Not recommended because some cases would be lost.
b. Not recommended because it would present a variety of problems.
c. For some topics, event-history analysis based on monthly dating requires the use of special files. Monthly dating analysis of employer/job changes for *heads* and *wives/"wives"* requires use of the *Work-History* file. Monthly event-history analysis of marital and childbirth events requires merging of special files (the *1985 Ego-Alter* file, the *Marital History* file, or the *Childbirth and Adoption History* file) with the *Cross-Year Family-Individual Response + Nonresponse Files*.

produces the same results as a larger but better suited PSID file. The PSID's *User Guide* provides more detailed illustrations of the types of analyses possible with each type of data file.

The *cross-year family-individual response + nonresponse files* permit longitudinal analysis of individuals and cross-sectional analysis of either families or individuals in any year covered by the study. These files have the important advantage of allowing the most direct means of addressing the complications of family composition change. *For these reasons, we urge the use of the* cross-year family-individual files *rather than the* cross-year family file *when undertaking analysis of multiple waves.* The higher initial processing costs from using these files are more than offset by the ease of understanding and properly managing the data. The multireel, *cross-year family-individual files*, however, may be too large for some computer installations, rendering this impossible.

The smaller *cross-year family file* offers the advantage of considerably fewer and somewhat shorter records. This file is limited in its representation of families, however. It allows cross-sectional analysis of families as of the most recent year of data. But analysis of families or individuals from prior years is not recommended. The *cross-year family-individual response + nonresponse files* must be used to obtain proper cross-sectional representation of families in years prior to the most recent one. The *cross-year family file* can be used for longitudinal analysis focusing on families that maintain the same head or include a female who remains a primary adult (*head* or *wife/"wife"*) over the period being analyzed. The analyst must proceed with supreme caution in undertaking longitudinal analysis with the *cross-year family file*, however, because family composition change can mean that *head* (*wife/"wife"*) in one year is a different person than *head* (*wife/"wife"*) in another year. The only advantage of the *cross-year family file* is its smaller size. Anything that can be done with that file can also be done with the *cross-year family-individual response file*.[10]

Data Analysis Examples

We provide five simple examples of analysis of PSID data: (a) an earnings regression based on a single year of data, (b) a pooled cross-sectional earnings regression based on two years of PSID data, (c) a longitudinal analysis showing the distribution of persons according to their number of years in poverty during a 10-year period, (d) a longitudinal measure of change in income following divorce, and (e) an intergenerational analysis correlating children's and parents' income. Additional details about these examples are provided in the *User Guide*. The calculations in these examples have been made both with SPSS-X and with OSIRIS.IV software; the two software packages produced no notable differences. Sampling error corrections for the regressions have been made with REPERR's balanced half-sample replications option; sampling error corrections for the other analyses have been made with PSALMS. Weights are used in the descriptive measures provided in Examples 3, 4, and 5. Weights are not used in Examples 1 and 2 to reflect the usual econometric assumption of perfect specification, in which case weights are irrelevant. This is an empirically testable assumption (DuMouchel & Duncan, 1983), but we have not pursued these tests here.

As a rule of thumb, it is useful to perform PSID analyses in two stages. First, subset from the data files only those records and variables intended for analysis. Then use this subset in the second stage for the actual calculations. In situations where it is difficult to fully anticipate all variables needed for the analysis, the preferable strategy can be to subset the sample with its full complement of variables in each record. The subsetting strategy can both substantially reduce the computer costs and ease the task of data management.

Example 1: Single-year cross-sectional regression. This example is a simple cross-sectional regression model of average hourly earnings. For this example, we use the 1968-1987 family-individual response file to estimate a 1986 earnings equation for prime-age (25-54) white male *heads* of households who are *sample members*. The dependent variable is the natural logarithm of 1986 average hourly earnings constructed from annual labor income and work hours reported in the 1987 interview. Only cases where 1986 hourly earnings were between $1.00 and $50.00 and 1986 work hours were between 250 and 4,000 are included in the analysis. These restrictions exclude workers with extreme values on wages or work hours. Independent variables include years of education and labor force experience. The unit of analysis is the individual. This regression is one typically formulated by labor economists, who hypothesize that education and work experience are the primary determinants of earnings.

A subset of the data is constructed from the *1968-1987 family-individual response file*. A record had to satisfy all of the conditions specified below to be retained in the subset (see PSID documentation for the 1987 interviewing year for details about these variables):

1987 PERSON NUMBER (V30002 = 1-169)
> to select sample members;

1987 RELATIONSHIP TO HEAD (V30556 = 10)
> to select individuals who headed households at the time of the 1987 interview;

1987 SEQUENCE NUMBER (V30555 = 1-20)
> to select individuals present in 1987 PSID family units at the time of the 1987 interview;

1987 RACE OF HEAD (V14612 = 1)
> to select whites;

1987 SEX OF INDIVIDUAL (V30560 = 1)
> to select males;

1987 AGE OF INDIVIDUAL (V30557 = 25-54)
> to select prime-age adults;

1987 REPORT OF HEAD'S 1986 ANNUAL WORK HOURS (V13745 = 250-4,000); and

1987 REPORT OF HEAD'S 1986 AVERAGE HOURLY EARNINGS (V14676 = 1-50).

The resulting sample size is 1,361 persons.

Working with the subset of records for these 1,361 men, the natural logarithm of hourly earnings is regressed on education and work experience. For this example, the measure of work experience that is used is "age minus (years of education completed plus 6)." There are more direct measures of work experience in PSID data, but labor economists have often used this proxy measure because of limited information on work experience in other data sets. This proxy measure treats all years following completion of education as years of full-time work (a less hazardous assumption for men than for women) and assumes all boys start school at age 6, with no repeating or skipping of grades. The measure of work experience also imposes a truncation of years of education from below at 10 years (to avoid careers beginning prior to age 16) and then subtracts the modified measure of years of education plus 6 from age. Experience enters the earnings equation both linearly and quadratically to capture the expected concavity of the life cycle earnings profile.

Equation 8.1 shows the results of the analysis. Years of education and experience are both highly significant predictors of hourly earnings. Together they explain 18% of the variance in wages. Standard errors of the regression coefficients corrected for design effects are shown in parentheses just below the coefficients, and standard errors assuming simple random sampling (the assumption of most regression software) are presented below them, in brackets.

$$Y = .510 + .107 * X_1 + .038 * X_2 - .0006 * X_3 \qquad [8.1]$$
$$(.007) \qquad (.008) \qquad (.0002)$$
$$[.115] \ [.006] \qquad [.008] \qquad [.0002]$$

$R^2 = .18$; standard error of the estimate $= .54$; Y: natural log of hourly earnings in 1986; X_1: years of education; X_2: experience; X_3: experience-squared.

Example 2: Multiyear pooled cross-sectional regression. The same earnings equation as in the previous example is calculated in this example but, this time, we pool together information for the most recent year and one past year and treat each year's data for a given individual as separate observations. This pooling approach often involves the use of many more waves of data, but our use of two years illustrates the important issues. With this pooling, the unit of analysis becomes the person-year, and we include any observation that passes the filter in *either* 1987 or 1986. Observations on individuals passing the filter in both years will be included twice, a task that requires a method (such as use of the commands SAVE OUTFILE, ADD FILES, and RENAME in SPSS-X) to write several records from a single record in one pass of the data. For this analysis, we use the *1968-1987 family-individual response + nonresponse files* so that 1986 interview year data collected for individuals who attrited between 1986 and 1987 can be included in the analysis.

Filters are used to select individuals who were white male *heads* of family units in either 1987 or 1986. The same restrictions on age, work hours, and earnings as in Example 1 apply to this analysis. Hence a person-year was included for 1987 if it satisfied the criteria listed in the previous example *or* for 1986 if it satisfied the analogous filter for 1986. The analogous filter for 1986 involved all of the conditions listed below (see PSID documentation for the 1986 interviewing year and for the 1987 interviewing year for details about these variables):

1986 RELATIONSHIP TO HEAD (V30518 = 10)
> to select individuals who headed households;

1986 SEQUENCE NUMBER (V30517 = 1-20)
> to select individuals present in 1986 PSID family units;

1986 RACE OF HEAD (V13565 = 1)
> to select whites;

1986 SEX OF INDIVIDUAL (V30522 = 1)
> to select males;

1986 AGE OF INDIVIDUAL (V30519 = 25-54)
> to select prime-age individuals;

1986 REPORT OF HEAD'S 1985 ANNUAL WORK HOURS (V12545 = 250-4,000); and

1986 REPORT OF HEAD'S 1985 AVERAGE HOURLY EARNINGS (V13629 = 1-50).

The resulting sample size, after pooling the valid observations in 1987 and 1986 together, is 2,739 (person-years).

As with the first example, the data are not weighted. Equation 8.2 shows the results of the analysis. (Standard errors are shown in the same way as in Example 1.) Both education and experience significantly increase one's earnings and explain 16% of the total variance in earnings.

$$Y = .517 + .103 * X_1 + .042 * X_2 - .0007 * X_3 \qquad [8.2]$$
$$(.006) \qquad (.007) \qquad (.0002)$$
$$[.082] \; [.005] \qquad [.006] \qquad [.0001]$$

$R^2 = .16$; standard error of the estimate = .55; Y: natural log of hourly earnings in 1986 or 1985; X_1: years of education; X_2: experience; X_3: experience-squared.

Example 3: Longitudinal measure of poverty. One of the relative strengths of the PSID sample is its coverage of the lower portion of the income distribution, a feature that enables analysts to investigate short- and long-term poverty. This example provides a simple descriptive statistic about the incidence of long-run poverty by counting the number of years in which each individual was below the poverty line between 1970 and 1979. This analysis uses the *1968-1987 family-individual response + nonresponse files* with the individual as the unit of analysis. The analysis is performed with weights because results will then be representative of the whole population. Because the sample is restricted to persons in family units interviewed between 1971 and 1980, the most recent (1980) individual weight (V30355) is used.

Three aspects of the data complicate this analysis. First, because family income and family needs are measured for the calendar year prior to the interviewing year, care must be taken in the selection of data waves. The waves of data needed to analyze poverty for the calendar-year period 1970 to 1979 are the interviewing years 1971 to 1980. Second, the sample is restricted to individuals living in PSID family units at the time of the interview in each of the 10 years. To avoid conceptual problems, we exclude individuals known to be deceased, in institutions, or attriters in any of the 10 years. These restrictions require the identification of individuals with

SEQUENCE NUMBER (V30326 = 1-20 and V30295 = 1-20 and V30257 = 1-20 and V30227 = 1-20 and V30197 = 1-20 and V30168 = 1-20 and V30145 = 1-20 and V30123 = 1-20 and V30096 = 1-20 and V30071 = 1-20).

Third, the PSID annual needs variables are adjusted to make them a closer approximation of the official poverty standard (see the "Idiosyncratic Aspects" chapter in the *User Guide* for details).

After adjusting the needs variables, the ratio of total family money income divided by annual family needs is calculated. A ratio with a value less than or equal to 1 indicates that the family is below the official poverty line. This poverty indicator is calculated for each of the 10 years. Because we are interested in figures representative of the population of the United States, the weights are used in the calculations. Results shown below indicate that about three fourths of the individuals were never in poverty during the 10-year period; 6% were in poverty for more than 5 years. Among those who did experience poverty over the 1970-1979 period, most were poor less than 4 years of the 10 years. Sampling error corrections indicate that the assumption of simple random sample understates the true standard errors in these calculations by from 40% to 140%.

Number of Years in Poverty between 1970-1979

	0	1	2	3	4	5	6	7	8	9	10	Total
%	75.8	9.6	4.5	2.6	1.5	1.4	1.4	0.7	0.9	0.9	0.7	100.0

(Total unweighted N = 11,291.)

Another way of portraying poverty experiences is with spells—consecutive years in which incomes are below the poverty line. With some care, the PSID data can be adapted to calculations based on continuous spells of poverty for PSID individuals (see Bane & Ellwood, 1986).

Example 4: Longitudinal estimate of change in income. Suppose we are interested in calculating change in family income for ex-wives following a divorce. Income in the year prior to the divorce is compared with that in the year after the divorce. This seems like a simple calculation, but it is complicated by three factors: (a) PSID income reports apply to the calendar year prior to the year of interview; (b) it is unclear whether the divorce occurred in the year of the interview or in the previous calendar year; and (c) PSID reports of family income span a full calendar year.

To obtain a large enough sample for our calculations, we use the *1968-1986 family-individual response + nonresponse files* and pool together divorces occurring roughly over a three-year time span, 1982-1985. We use PSID variables indicating marital change; these are generated from information on marital status at the time of interview in the current wave and in the prior wave. We examine divorces occurring between times of interview in 1982 and 1983, between times of interview in 1983 and 1984, or between times of interview in 1984 and 1985. Taking divorces between times of interview in 1982 and 1983 as an example, we look to the 1982 interviewing year for a 1981 calendar-year report of predivorce income, and we look to the 1984 interviewing year for the 1983 calendar-year report of postdivorce income. This approach helps minimize problems of pre- and postdivorce measures of annual income including time partly in and partly out of the divorced state, while not moving so far from the point of divorce as to have the calculations confounded by remarriage.

To be included in the sample, a woman had to be a *wife/"wife"* at time of interview in wave t − 1 and report (in interviewing wave t) a divorce having occurred between wave t − 1 and wave t, where t includes 1983, 1984, and 1985. Further, the woman must have been present in the study in waves t − 1, t, and t + 1. If more than one divorce was reported, only the first was included in this analysis. To maximize case counts and minimize attrition losses, the *1968-1987 family-individual response + nonresponse files* are used. To select the sample for this analysis, a number of variables were used in the filter. We list the filter variables relevant for the divorces reported in the 1983 interviewing wave in italics and those relevant for divorces reported in either the 1984 or 1985 interviewing wave in brackets (see PSID documentation for the 1983 interviewing year, 1984 interviewing year, 1985 interviewing year, and 1987 interviewing year for details about these variables):

RELATIONSHIP TO HEAD (*V30389* [V30416, V30447] = 2, 20, or 22)
    to select women who were *wives/"wives"*;
MARITAL STATUS CHANGE (*V9420* [V11066, V12427] = 3 or 6)
    to select those reporting a divorce between 1982 and 1983, 1983 and 1984, or 1984 and 1985;
SEQUENCE NUMBER (*V30388* [V30415, V30446] = 1-20)
    to select those present in family units in the year *prior* to the divorce (when the predivorce family income is reported);
SEQUENCE NUMBER (*V30415* [V30446, V30481] = 1-20)
    to select those present in family units the year the divorce is reported; and
SEQUENCE NUMBER (*V30446* [V30481, V30517] = 1-20)
    to select those present in family units the year *after* the divorce.

The relevant measures of family income before divorce (*V8689*, V9375, V11022) reflect the 1981-1983 calendar years as reported in the 1982-1984 interviews (1981 is the last complete predivorce calendar year for the divorces reported in the 1983 interviews). The relevant measures of postdivorce family income (*V11022*, V12371, V13623) reflect the 1983-1985 calendar years as reported in the

1984-1986 interviews. Incomes are adjusted to 1985 dollars using the Consumer Price Index, and the calculations are weighted by individual-level weights as of 1984, 1985, or 1986 (whichever is the interviewing wave used to obtain the measure of postdivorce income). Assignment of pre- and postdivorce income amounts to a series of conditional statements of the following form: If the woman first reported a divorce in 1983, then take family income reported in the 1982 interview as the measure of predivorce family income and the income reported in the 1984 interview as the postdivorce family income. Similar statements can be constructed for the divorces reported in the 1984 and 1985 interviews.

The sample consists of 301 ex-wives and ex-cohabitors. Results indicate that the median drop in family income for women following divorce was $11,888. We did not attempt to calculate a standard error for this estimate.

Example 5: Intergenerational income correlation. This example calculates the simple product-moment correlation between the income of a person's parental family and the person's own income after he or she has left home. The sample consists of persons who were children in the family (or an institution, such as college) at age 18 and who were also later observed as *head* or *wife/"wife"* in their own families at age 30. The correlation coefficient gives us a measure of intergenerational income mobility.

As the first step, a subset of individuals aged 30 in at least one of the 1980-1987 interviews is selected from the *1968-1987 family-individual response + nonresponse files.* (This also gives us the set of persons potentially observed at age 18 in the 1968-1975 interviews.) Getting the final sample involves somewhat more complicated coding than can be handled in this initial filter statement and thus is done as a later step. To pass the filter in the initial step, a record had to satisfy the combination of the following conditions:

PERSON NUMBER (V30002 = 1-169)
    [to select *sample members*] and
AGE OF INDIVIDUAL (V30328 = 30 or V30359 = 30 or V30390 = 30 or V30417
    = 30 or V30448 = 30 or V30483 = 30 or V30519 = 30 or V30557 = 30).

The resulting sample size is 2,039. A further filtering is accomplished by selecting only those who were *head* or *wife/"wife"* of a family at age 30 and who were also children in a family or institution 12 years previously (thus at age 18). This is done using RELATIONSHIP TO HEAD, SEQUENCE NUMBER, and AGE variables. These additional requirements reduce the sample to its final size of 1,542. Note that "age 30" information may come from any of the interviews 1980 to 1987 and "age 18" information from any of the interviews 1968 to 1975. The filtering retains the years the person was ages 30 and 18 so that the income (and other) information for that person from those years can be analyzed.

Using the PSID measure of family money income as the base, we subtract federal income taxes (included as variables in the PSID), subtract social security/FICA payroll taxes of the *head* and *wife/"wife"* (constructed from the *head* and *wife/"wife"* earnings measures in the PSID and statutory rates and bases), and add the money value of food stamps (also included as variables in the PSID). All incomes are then converted to 1987 dollars using the appropriate year's Consumer Price Index. The computation is weighted by the person's individual-level weight variable for the year when he or she was age 30.

The resulting correlation coefficient between the child's parental and own adult income (both in log form) is 0.23. The assumption of simple random sampling understates the true standard errors by 78%. This is consistent with other studies using U.S. data in indicating a high degree of intergenerational income mobility. A recent careful study by Solon (1990) using the PSID data, in which the author made corrections for bias due to measurement error, found a much higher intergenerational income correlation of 0.4.

This is but a small sampling of the wide possibilities for analyzing PSID data. A complete bibliography is available upon request from PSID staff. The next chapter explains details about obtaining additional information on research using the PSID, further information about topics covered in PSID questionnaires, and the data themselves.

Notes

1. The exception is the child who left the parental family to set up a separate household, attrited, and then moved back to the parental family.

2. The exceptions include TYPE OF INDIVIDUAL RECORD and WHY NONRESPONSE, plus several of the summary variables at the end of the individual-level portion of each record.

3. Entry into the PSID can occur either by marriage, by coresidency, or by being born to a *sample member* while that *sample member* is in the study.

4. The exceptions are 1968 FAMILY ID, PERSON NUMBER, TYPE OF INDIVIDUAL RECORD, and WHY NONRESPONSE.

5. Not included among these reasons is the notion that the PSID sample has "aged" over time and no longer represents young families and individuals. This notion is false because the PSID does have a mechanism for adding new families and individuals (births) to the sample just as new families and individuals are added to the U.S. population.

6. Some caution is warranted regarding the compatibility of weights across waves. In 1968-1989 and subsequent cross-year files, weights are scaled identically across waves. However, in all cross-year files with data no more recent than the 1988 wave, there is one exception to identical scaling: the 1968 weight was scaled at twice the size of the weights of subsequent years. Analysts wanting to scale weights identically in cross-year files with the most recent year being 1984-1988 should cut the 1968 weight in half.

7. The complex nature of the sample makes it impossible to do this using a random number table or similar device.

8. In the description of the ranges, "wave 1" refers to 1968 for the main PSID sample and to 1990 for the *Latino subsample* added in 1990.

9. These include nonsample individuals recontacted after attriting in prior waves, nonsample individuals in responding family units, and *movers-in* who did not satisfy the PSID definition of a *sample member.*

10. To analyze families with the same family unit *head* over a given period using the cross-year family-individual files, one selects individuals whose SEQUENCE NUMBER equals 1 over the given period.

9. Getting Started

Ordering Data Files and Documentation

Public-release files. With only a few exceptions (see "Special Restricted Files" in Table 7.1 for exceptions), PSID data files are available to the public through the Inter-University Consortium for Political and Social Research (ICPSR).[1] More than 270 academic institutions are currently members of that organization. Member institutions pay a fixed annual fee, which provides access to all data tapes in the archive. Requests for data at member institutions are coordinated through an Official Representative

(OR) at that institution. Data are available with a per-item charge to users at nonmember institutions.[2] The ICPSR copies the data onto magnetic tapes with technical specifications and in data formats that are compatible with the user's installation. To obtain more information about the ICPSR, any data in its holdings, or a copy of its *Guide to Resources and Services* contact Janet Vavra, ICPSR, P.O. Box 1248, Ann Arbor, Michigan 48106; phone (313) 763-5010.

Historically, PSID data files have been released only on magnetic tape. The ICPSR has released a test CD-ROM containing the rectangular *1968-1987 family-individual response and nonresponse files*. An ASCII version of these two files has been mastered onto two CD-ROMs (they cannot both fit on a single CD). The response file is on one CD-ROM and the *nonresponse file* on the other. SAS and SPSS-X statement files are also on the disks.

When ordering the public-release PSID files, it is almost always advantageous to order the most recent version of the file. Information from prior waves is also on the most recent file. With the advent of the *cross-year family-individual nonresponse file*, prior waves can be completely represented with the main PSID files by concatenating the most recent response and nonresponse cross-year family-individual files. The PSID staff corrects any errors discovered in prior waves of data when it merges them with subsequent waves. This produces some change in values of prior variables, including an occasional change in the identifiers for individuals. Although the ICPSR does not keep versions of PSID files that predate the most recent one, interested data users can request earlier files from the ICPSR, which then contacts the PSID staff for access in making copies of the earlier files.

Special restricted files. To obtain information about the special restricted files and procedures for acquiring access to them, contact Greg Duncan directly at (313) 763-5186.

User Guide

The project staff developed a comprehensive *User Guide* for the data in 1983, with a revised version projected for 1992. The *User*

Guide sums up, in one volume, significant features and idiosyncracies of the data and provides step-by-step guidelines and examples of analysis with PSID data. A profile is given of the data structure, and recurrent problematic or complex aspects of the data are summarized and explained. Perhaps the most useful part of the *User Guide* is an alphabetical list of variables, with the variable numbers for each year and indications of any problems of year-to-year comparability. This part of the *User Guide* is revised and updated annually. Like the PSID documentation and data files, the *User Guide* is advertised and disseminated by the ICPSR.

Bibliography and User Survey

The PSID has assembled and continually researches and updates a bibliography intended as a comprehensive reference source for all published articles, books, and monographs that use PSID data. In all, 26 major economic, demographic, and sociological journals as well as major social science indexes are searched once a year. The PSID staff also routinely search NBER working papers and papers presented at the Population Association of America meetings. Working papers from other sources, dissertations, and government reports are added to the bibliographic listing when they come to our attention. (We urge data users to send us copies of their publications, working papers, and research reports to assist us in keeping up to date about work being done with the data. These can be sent to the address listed in the "Staff Assistance" section that follows.) The approximately 700 individuals who are on the PSID's computer-based user mailing list are periodically sent copies of the bibliography, along with a request for assistance in revising and/or updating the listings. Copies of the bibliography are available from the PSID staff upon request.

To maintain active communication with those on the PSID's ever-growing data user list, the PSID periodically circulates a newsletter informing data users about new data files and services, new members on the Board of Overseers, and recent PSID activities and developments. Surveys to assess PSID data users' needs and data dissemination preferences are also done periodically.

Staff Assistance

PSID staff provide assistance to data users who have questions or problems remaining *after a diligent search* of the study's documentation and *User Guide*. This activity can be of assistance to the study as well because it can alert PSID staff to areas needing more attention either via documentation or via methodological changes. Obtain assistance as follows:

(1) Contact PSID Staff:
Institute for Social Research, P.O. Box 1248, Ann Arbor, Michigan 48106
PHONE: (313) 763-5166; FAX: (313) 747-4575
BITNET:USERPSID@UMICHUM
INTERNET:PSID_STAFF@UM.CC.UMICH.EDU

(2) Describe the problem in nontechnical terms but with sufficient detail for the recipient of your message to understand what type of assistance is needed and what type of knowledge about the PSID would best address the problem. The best suited staff member can then respond to your question or problem.

Again, we urge data users to obtain and consult the PSID documentation and *User Guide* before contacting the study for assistance. A great deal of effort goes into creating and maintaining those publications, they are quite comprehensive, and they are designed to address most questions that arise.

Good luck!

Notes

1. A complete listing and brief description of all data collections in the ICPSR holdings can be found in the *Guide to Resources and Services*, published annually by ICPSR.

2. Individuals at nonmember institutions, persons who are uncertain whether they are at member institutions, and persons not knowing the name of their Official Representative should contact the ICPSR directly.

References

Bane, M., & Ellwood, D. (1986). Slipping into and out of poverty: The dynamics of spells. *Journal of Human Resources, 21*(1), 1-23.

Becketti, S., Gould, W., Lillard, L., & Welch, F. (1988). The PSID after fourteen years: An evaluation. *Journal of Labor Economics, 6*(4), 472-492.

Bound, J., Brown, C., Duncan, G. J., & Rodgers, W. (1989). *Measurement error in cross-sectional and longitudinal labor market surveys: Results from two validation studies* (Working Paper No. 2884). Cambridge, MA: National Bureau of Economic Research.

Bound, J., & Krueger, A. B. (1989). *The extent of measurement error in longitudinal earnings data: Do two wrongs make a right?* (Working Paper No. 2885). Cambridge, MA: National Bureau of Economic Research.

Curtin, R., Juster, F. T., & Morgan, J. (1988). Survey estimates of wealth: An assessment of quality. In R. Lipsey & H. Tice (Eds.), *The measurement of saving, investment and wealth.* Chicago: University of Chicago Press.

DuMouchel, W. H., & Duncan, G. J. (1983). Using sample survey weights in multiple regression analyses of stratified samples. *Journal of the American Statistical Association, 78,* 535-543.

Duncan, G. J., & Hill, D. (1989). Assessing the quality of household panel survey data: The case of the PSID. *Journal of Business and Economic Statistics, 7*(4), 441-451.

Duncan, G. J., & Hill, M. (1985). Conception of longitudinal households: Fertile or futile? *Journal of Economic and Social Measurement, 3,* 361-375.

Duncan, G. J., & Hoffman, S. D. (1991). Teenage underclass behavior and subsequent poverty: Have the rules changed? In C. Jencks & P. Peterson (Eds.), *The urban underclass* (pp. 155-174). Washington, DC: Brookings Institution.

Duncan, G. J., Juster, T. F., & Morgan, J. N. (1984). The role of panel studies in a world of scarce research resources. In S. Sudman & M. A. Spaeth (Eds.), *The collection and analysis of economic and consumer behavior data: In memory of Robert Ferber.* Urbana: University of Illinois, Bureau of Economic and Business Research and Survey Research Laboratory.

Fuller, W. G. (1986). *PC CARP.* Ames: Iowa State University.

Hidiroglou, M. A., Fuller, W. A., & Hickman, R. D. (1980). *SUPER CARP.* Ames: Iowa State University.

Hill, D. (1987). Response errors around the seam: Analysis of change in a panel with overlapping reference periods. In American Statistical Association, *Proceedings of the section on survey research method.* Washington, DC: ASA.

Hill, M. S. (1981). Some illustrative design effects: Proper sampling errors versus simple random sample assumptions. In M. S. Hill, D. H. Hill, & J. N. Morgan (Eds.), *Five thousand American families: Patterns of economic progress* (Vol. 9). Ann Arbor: University of Michigan, Survey Research Center, Institute for Social Research.

88

Hill, M. S., & Hill, D. (1986). Labor force transitions: A comparison of unemployment estimates from two longitudinal surveys. In *American Statistical Association, Proceedings of the section on survey research method.* Washington, DC: ASA.

Inter-University Consortium for Political and Social Research (ICPSR). [Updated annually]. *Guide to resources and services.* Ann Arbor, MI: Author.

Kalton, G. (1979). Practical methods for estimating survey sampling errors. *Bulletin of the International Statistical Institute, 47*(3), 495-514.

Kalton, G. (1986). *Including nonsample persons in PSID analyses.* Commissioned paper prepared for the Board-of-Overseers meetings of the Panel Study of Income Dynamics.

Kish, L. (1965). *Survey sampling.* New York: John Wiley.

Kish, L., & Frankel, M. R. (1970). Balanced repeated replicators for standard errors. *Journal of American Statistical Association, 65,* 1071-1094.

Lansing, J. B., & Morgan, J. N. (1971). *Economic survey methods.* Ann Arbor: University of Michigan, Institute for Social Research.

Lillard, L. (1989). Sample dynamics: Some behavioral issues. In D. Kasprzyk, G. Duncan, G. Kalton, & M. P. Singh (Eds.), *Panel surveys* (pp. 497-511). New York: John Wiley.

Lillard, L., & Waite, L. (1989). Panel versus retrospective data on marital histories: Lessons from the PSID. In H. V. Beaton, D. A. Ganni, & D. T. Frankel (Compilers), *Individuals and families in transition: Understanding change through longitudinal data.* Washington, DC: U.S. Bureau of the Census.

Little, R. (1989). *Sampling weights in the PSID: Issues and comments.* Commissioned paper prepared for the fall Board of Overseers meeting of the Panel Study of Income Dynamics.

McCarthy, P. J. (1966). *Replication: An approach to the analysis of data from complex surveys* (Series 2, No. 14). Washington, DC: Public Health Service.

Shah, B. V. (1981). *SESUDAAN: Standard errors program for computing of standardized rates from sample survey data.* Research Triangle Park, NC: Research Triangle Institute.

Shah, B. V., La Vange, L., Barnwell, B. G., Killinger, J. E., & Wheeless, S. C. (1989). *SUDAAN: Procedures for descriptive statistics.* Research Triangle Park, NC: Research Triangle Institute.

Solon, G. (1990). *Intergenerational income mobility in the U.S.* Unpublished manuscript, University of Michigan, Ann Arbor.

Survey Research Center, Economic Behavior Program. (1984). *User guide to the Panel Study of Income Dynamics.* Ann Arbor: University of Michigan, Inter-University Consortium for Political and Social Research.

Survey Research Center, Economic Behavior Program. (1986). *A Panel Study of Income Dynamics: Procedures and tape codes 1984 interviewing year, wave XVII.* Ann Arbor: University of Michigan, Institute for Social Research.

U.S. Bureau of the Census. (1983). *Money income of households, families, and persons in the United States, 1981* (Current Population Report 137, Ser. P-60). Washington, DC: Government Printing Office.

U.S. Bureau of the Census. (1985). *Economic characteristics of households in the United States: Fourth quarter 1983* (Current Population Report, Ser. P-70-83-4). Washington, DC: Government Printing Office.

Wolter, K. (1985). *Introduction to variance estimation.* New York: Springer-Verlag.

About the Author

Martha S. Hill, an economic demographer by training, is Associate Research Scientist at the Survey Research Center, Institute for Social Research, University of Michigan. For more than a decade, she has been the PSID's chief demographer and family economics specialist. Her research covers topics relating to the family, labor market behavior, and economic well-being, viewed from the perspective of large, national, longitudinal data sets. The specific topics she has examined include living arrangements and household formation, marital stability, child support, the dynamics of poverty and welfare across time and generations, time use, unemployment, and wage determinants.